PRISM
READING
Student's Book

| Intro

Kate Adams
Sabina Ostrowska

with
Christina Cavage

CAMBRIDGE
UNIVERSITY PRESS

CAMBRIDGE
UNIVERSITY PRESS

University Printing House, Cambridge CB2 8BS, United Kingdom

One Liberty Plaza, 20th Floor, New York, NY 10006, USA

477 Williamstown Road, Port Melbourne, VIC 3207, Australia

314–321, 3rd Floor, Plot 3, Splendor Forum, Jasola District Centre, New Delhi – 110025, India

103 Penang Road, #05–06/07, Visioncrest Commercial, Singapore 238467

Cambridge University Press is part of the University of Cambridge.

It furthers the University's mission by disseminating knowledge in the pursuit of education, learning and research at the highest international levels of excellence.

Information on this title: www.cambridge.org/9781009251327

© Cambridge University Press & Assessment 2022

First published 2018
Update published 2022

20 19 18 17 16 15 14 13 12 11 10 9 8 7 6 5 4 3 2 1

Printed in Mexico by Litográfica Ingramex, S.A. de C.V.

A catalogue record for this publication is available from the British Library

ISBN 978-1-009-25132-7 Prism Reading Intro Student's Book with Digital Pack
ISBN 978-1-108-45529-9 Prism Reading Intro Teacher's Manual

CONTENTS

SCOPE AND SEQUENCE

UNIT	READING PASSAGES	KEY READING SKILLS	ADDITIONAL READING SKILLS	
1 PEOPLE *Academic Disciplines* Communications / Sociology	1 My Profile: Jeremy Lin (social media profile) 2 A Very Tall Man! (article)	Previewing	Understanding key vocabulary Skimming Scanning to find information Reading for details Taking notes Synthesizing	
2 CLIMATE *Academic Disciplines* Meteorology / Geography	1 The Coldest City in the World (article) 2 Cuba Weather (website)	Scanning to find information Taking notes in a chart	Understanding key vocabulary Using your knowledge Previewing Reading for details Synthesizing	
3 LIFESTYLE *Academic Disciplines* Anthropology / Education	1 Meet the Kombai (book review) 2 Class schedule and email (mixed text types)	Annotating	Understanding key vocabulary Using your knowledge Predicting content using visuals Scanning to find information Reading for main ideas Previewing Reading for details Synthesizing	
4 PLACES *Academic Disciplines* Geography / History	1 A World History of Maps: Muhammad al-Idrisi's World Map (book excerpts) 2 The Maldives: An Overview (country profile)	Reading for main ideas	Understanding key vocabulary Previewing Annotating Scanning to find information Reading for details Using your knowledge Taking notes Synthesizing	

LANGUAGE DEVELOPMENT	WATCH AND LISTEN	SPECIAL FEATURES
Family vocabulary Nouns and verbs Singular and plural nouns	Thailand's Moken Fishermen	Critical Thinking Collaboration
Nouns and adjectives Noun phrases	The Growing Ice Cap	Critical Thinking Collaboration
Collocations for free-time activities Time expressions	Panama's Kuna People	Critical Thinking Collaboration
Superlative adjectives Noun phrases with *of* Vocabulary for places	The *Cenotes* of Mexico	Critical Thinking Collaboration

UNIT	READING PASSAGES	KEY READING SKILLS	ADDITIONAL READING SKILLS	

5 JOBS
 	
Academic Disciplines
Business / Career Services
	1 Find_my_job.com
	(website)
	2 Emails about jobs
	(emails)
		Reading for details	Understanding key
			  vocabulary
			Using your knowledge
			Previewing
			Scanning to find
			  information
			Taking notes
			Reading for main ideas
			Synthesizing	

**6 HOMES AND
BUILDINGS**
 	
Discipline
Architecture / Engineering
	1 _Architect's World_:
	Expert Interview
	(printed interview)
	2 Skyscrapers:
	Buildings that Touch
	the Sky
	(report)
		Predicting content using
		visuals
			Understanding key
			  vocabulary
			Using your knowledge
			Scanning to find
			  information
			Reading for main ideas
			Reading for details
			Annotating
			Synthesizing	

**7 FOOD AND
CULTURE**
 	
Academic Disciplines
History / Sociology
	1 Tea: A World History
	(article)
	2 10 of the Best by
	Cuisine
	(travel guide)
		Taking notes	Understanding key
			  vocabulary
			Using your knowledge
			Previewing
			Reading for main ideas
			Scanning to find
			  information
			Reading for details
			Synthesizing	

8 TRANSPORTATION
 	
Academic Disciplines
Engineering / Urban Planning
	1 Transportation Survey
	(survey)
	2 Transportation in
	Bangkok
	(report)
		Skimming	Understanding key
			  vocabulary
			Previewing
			Scanning to find
			  information
			Reading for details
			Using your knowledge
			Reading for main ideas
			Annotating
			Synthesizing	

LANGUAGE DEVELOPMENT	WATCH AND LISTEN	SPECIAL FEATURES
Vocabulary for jobs Adjective phrases	Utah's Bingham Mine	Critical Thinking Collaboration
Pronouns Vocabulary for buildings Adjectives for buildings	To Build the Tallest	Critical Thinking Collaboration
Vocabulary about food Count and noncount nouns	Goat Cheese	Critical Thinking Collaboration
Quantifiers Transportation collocations	Modern Subways	Critical Thinking Collaboration

HOW *PRISM READING* WORKS

① READING

Receptive, language, and analytical skills

Students improve their reading skills through a sequence of proven activities. First they study key vocabulary to prepare for each reading and to develop academic reading skills. Then they work on synthesis exercises in the second reading that prepare students for college classrooms. Language Development sections teach vocabulary, collocations, and language structure.

READING 1

PREPARING TO READ

1 UNDERSTANDING KEY VOCABULARY **Read the sentences. Choose the best definition for the word or phrase in bold.**

1 The **traffic** is moving slowly. There are a lot of cars on the road.
   a the cars, trucks, etc., driving on the road
   b the time it takes to get somewhere
2 When does the **train** get into the station? I need to be at work by 9 a.m.
   a a long, thin type of car that travels on tracks
   b a route or way for traveling from one place to another
3 I take the **subway** to work. I only have to go two stops.
   a a place for people to walk along the road
   b trains that travel underground, usually in a city
4 Many children learn to ride **bikes**. It's a fun and easy way to travel.
   a a type of transportation with two wheels that you sit on and move by turning two pedals
   b a type of transportation with four wheels and an engine.
5 I paid a **taxi** driver to take me from the airport to the city.
   a a place for planes to land and people to get on planes
   b a car with a driver who you pay to take you somewhere
6 My son takes the **bus** to school with other kids from his class.
   a a big type of car that takes many people around a city
   b a small car with three wheels

TRANSPORTATION IN *BANGKOK*

REPORT

Introduction

1 This **report** shows the **results** of a survey about transportation in Bangkok. Over eight million people live in the city. The pie chart (Figure 1) shows the most popular types of transportation in Bangkok. It shows the percentage[1] of people who use each type of transportation to get to work or school.

Public Transportation

2 Every day, thousands of people use public and private transportation. A popular form of public transportation is the SkyTrain. People take public transportation so they don't have to drive themselves. Twenty-one percent of the population of Bangkok takes the SkyTrain to work or school. Another form of public transportation in the city is the bus. Eighteen percent of people who live in Bangkok **take** buses. People **prefer** buses to tuk-tuks because buses cost less money. Only 8% of people use tuk-tuks to get to work or school.

[1]percentage (n) how many out of 100

Private Transportation

3 Most people in Bangkok use private transportation. They **drive** their own cars. Fourteen percent of people **ride** motorcycles to get to work or take children to school. Only 3% walk to work, and only 2% bike to work. Most places of work are too far away to walk or bike to.

Traffic

4 There is a lot of traffic in Bangkok. The roads are full of different types of vehicles[2] (cars, motorcycles, tuk-tuks, etc.). Twenty-three percent of people drive a car to work or school. Most people **spend** more than one hour every day traveling because the traffic is so bad. Almost 35% of people are late because of traffic jams. However, there are no traffic jams on the river. Eleven percent of people take the water taxi.

[2]vehicles (n) things such as cars or buses that take people from one place to another, especially using roads

(1) SkyTrain
(2) on foot (3) bike
(4) car
(5) bus
(6) tuk-tuk
(7) water taxi
(8) motorcycle

Figure 1: Transportation use in Bangkok

The busy Bangkok SkyTrain

② MORE READING

Critical thinking and collaboration

Multiple critical thinking activities prepare students for exercises that focus on academic reading skills. Collaboration activities help develop higher-level thinking skills, oral communication, and understanding of different opinions. By working with others students, they become better prepared for real life social and academic situations.

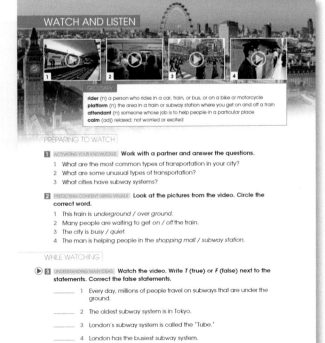

③ VIDEO

Summarizing the unit

Each unit ends with a carefully selected video clip that piques student interest and pulls together what they have learned. Video lessons also develop key skills such as prediction, comprehension, and discussion.

PREPARE YOUR STUDENTS TO SUCCEED IN COLLEGE CLASSES AND BEYOND

Capturing interest

- Students experience the topics and expand their vocabulary through captivating readings and videos that pull together everything they have learned in the unit, while developing academic reading and critical thinking skills.

- Teachers can deliver effective and engaging lessons using Presentation Plus.

Building confidence

- *Prism Reading* teaches skills that enable students to read, understand, and analyze university texts with confidence.

- Readings from a variety of academic disciplines in different formats (essays, articles, websites, etc.) expose and prepare students to comprehend real-life text they may face in or outside the classroom.

Extended learning

- The Digital Workbook has one extra reading and additional practice for each unit. Automated feedback gives autonomy to students while allowing teachers to spend less time grading and more time teaching.

Research-based

- Topics, vocabulary, academic and critical thinking skills to build students' confidence and prepare them for college courses were shaped by conversations with teachers at over 500 institutions.

- Carefully selected vocabulary students need to be successful in college are based on the General Service List, the Academic Word List, and the Cambridge English Corpus.

PATH TO
BETTER LEARNING

CLEAR LEARNING OBJECTIVES

Every unit begins with clear learning objectives.

RICH CONTENT

Highly visual unit openers with discussion questions are engaging opportunities for previewing unit themes.

SCAFFOLDED INSTRUCTION

Activities and tasks support the development of critical thinking skills.

COLLABORATIVE GROUP WORK

Critical thinking is followed by collaborative tasks and activities for the opportunity to apply new skills. Tasks are project-based and require teamwork, research, and presentation. These projects are similar to ones in an academic program.

CRITICAL THINKING

After reading, targeted questions help develop critical thinking skills. The questions range in complexity to prepare students for higher-level course work.

EXTENDED LEARNING OPPORTUNITIES

In-class projects and online activities extend learning beyond the textbook.

BETTER LEARNING

WHAT MAKES *PRISM READING* SPECIAL: CRITICAL THINKING

BLOOM'S TAXONOMY

Prism Reading prepares students for college coursework by explicitly teaching a full range of critical thinking skills. Critical thinking exercises appear in every unit of every level, organized according to the taxonomy developed by Benjamin Bloom.

Critical thinking exercises are highlighted in a special box and indicates which skills the students are learning.

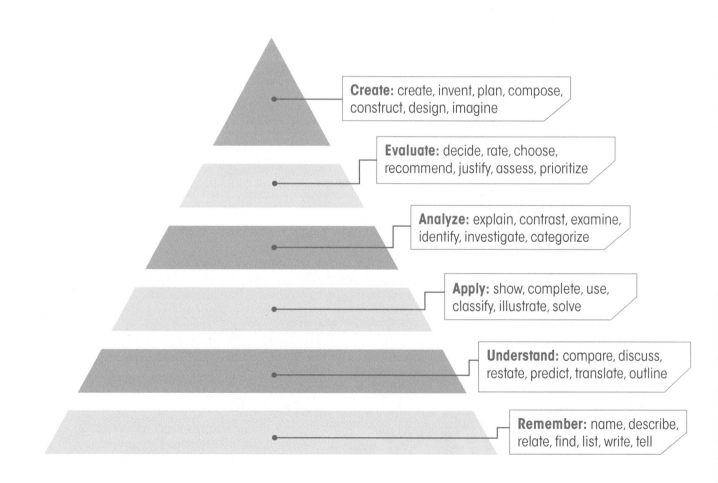

⚙ CRITICAL THINKING

7 SYNTHESIZING Work with a partner. Use ideas from Reading 1 and Reading 2 to answer the questions.

APPLY
What is the most popular way to get to work in Bangkok? Why do you think that is?

ANALYZE
If you lived in Bangkok, what transportation would you use? Why?

EVALUATE
Why is it important for cities to know how people get to work?

Create: create, invent, plan, compose, construct, design, imagine

Evaluate: decide, rate, choose, recommend, justify, assess, prioritize

Analyze: explain, contrast, examine, identify, investigate, categorize

Apply: show, complete, use, classify, illustrate, solve

Understand: compare, discuss, restate, predict, translate, outline

Remember: name, describe, relate, find, list, write, tell

HIGHER-ORDER THINKING SKILLS

Create, Evaluate, Analyze

Students' academic success depends on their ability to derive knowledge from collected data, make educated judgments, and deliver insightful presentations. *Prism Reading* helps students gain these skills with activities that teach them the best solution to a problem, and develop arguments for a discussion or presentation.

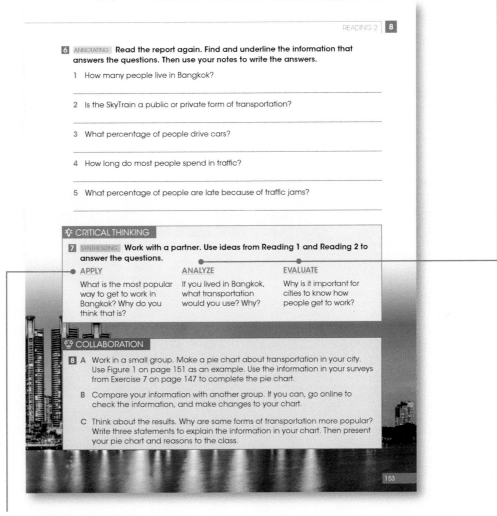

READING 2 8

6 ANNOTATING **Read the report again. Find and underline the information that answers the questions. Then use your notes to write the answers.**

1 How many people live in Bangkok?

2 Is the SkyTrain a public or private form of transportation?

3 What percentage of people drive cars?

4 How long do most people spend in traffic?

5 What percentage of people are late because of traffic jams?

✧ CRITICAL THINKING

7 SYNTHESIZING **Work with a partner. Use ideas from Reading 1 and Reading 2 to answer the questions.**

APPLY
What is the most popular way to get to work in Bangkok? Why do you think that is?

ANALYZE
If you lived in Bangkok, what transportation would you use? Why?

EVALUATE
Why is it important for cities to know how people get to work?

✿ COLLABORATION

8 A Work in a small group. Make a pie chart about transportation in your city. Use Figure 1 on page 151 as an example. Use the information in your surveys from Exercise 7 on page 147 to complete the pie chart.

B Compare your information with another group. If you can, go online to check the information, and make changes to your chart.

C Think about the results. Why are some forms of transportation more popular? Write three statements to explain the information in your chart. Then present your pie chart and reasons to the class.

153

LOWER-ORDER THINKING SKILLS

Apply, Understand, Remember

Students need to be able to recall information, comprehend it, and see its use in new contexts. These skills form the foundation for all higher-order thinking, and *Prism Reading* develops them through exercises that teach note-taking, comprehension, and the ability to distill information from charts.

PEOPLE

LEARNING OBJECTIVES

Key Reading Skill	Previewing
Additional Reading Skills	Understanding key vocabulary; skimming; scanning to find information; reading for details; taking notes; synthesizing
Language Development	Family vocabulary; nouns and verbs; singular and plural nouns

ACTIVATE YOUR KNOWLEDGE

Work with a partner. Ask and answer the questions.

1 What is your name?
2 Where do you live?
3 Do you have a job? What do you do?
4 Do you study? What do you study?

PREPARING TO READ

1 UNDERSTANDING KEY VOCABULARY **Read the words and examples in the box. Then write the bold words from the box in the sentences.**

words	examples
languages	Spanish, Urdu, Russian
city	New York City, Montreal
date of birth	May 4, 1998
country	United States, Mexico
job	teacher, doctor
hobbies	reading, playing the piano, running

1   London is a very big _____ in England. Many people live there.

2   I speak three _____ : Turkish, Arabic, and English.

3   Morocco is a _____ in North Africa. It is next to Algeria and Spain.

4   My _____ is July 7, 1997.

5   I have a great _____ . I am a teacher.

6   I have many _____ . I like running, reading, and playing the piano.

What are your hobbies?

SKILLS

PREVIEWING

Previewing means looking at a text before you read it. When you preview a text, look at the text and think about these questions:

1   Are there photos?
2   What is in the photos?
3   What is the title of the text?
4   Where is the text from? (a book? a magazine? a web page?)

2 PREVIEWING **Look at the photos and the text on pages 18-19. Ask and answer the questions with a partner.**

1   Read the title. What is a profile?
2   Where can you find profiles?
3   What do the photos show?
4   Who do you think Jeremy Lin is?
5   What does he like?

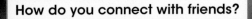

How do you connect with friends?

FRIEND*file*

MY PROFILE

Jeremy Lin

MY PERSONAL INFORMATION ▶

First name	Jeremy
Last name	Lin
Date of birth	August 23, 1988
City	Torrance, California
Country	United States
Languages	English, Mandarin
Job	Basketball player

(1) ▶

Email	jeremy.lin@cup.org

(2) ▶

Mother	Shirley
Father	Gie-Ming
Brothers	Josh and Joseph

(3) ▶

High school	Palo Alto
College	Harvard University

(4) ▶

Hobbies	playing the piano, playing video games
Other interests	helping young people

(5) ▶

I'm Jeremy Lin. My mother and father are from Taiwan. I speak two languages: English and Mandarin. I am a basketball player. I have played on many basketball teams in the United States. My brothers' names are Josh and Joseph. They like basketball, too. I also like playing the piano and playing video games.

3 SKIMMING **Read the text on pages 18–19 quickly. Write the words from the box in the blank spaces in the text.**

> Contact information   My hobbies and interests
> Education   My family   My life

4 SCANNING TO FIND INFORMATION **Read the text again. Circle the correct words to make true sentences.**

1 Jeremy is from *Taiwan / the United States*.
2 Jeremy's brothers like *basketball / video games*.
3 Jeremy's hobbies are *playing the piano and video games / playing the piano and basketball*.
4 Helping young people is Jeremy's other *job / interest*.
5 Shirley is Jeremy's *sister / mother*.
6 Gie-Ming is Jeremy's *brother / father*.
7 Jeremy's email address is *cup@jeremy.lin / jeremy.lin@cup.org*.
8 He went to *Harvard University / Boston University*.

5 READING FOR DETAILS **Read the summary and circle the correct words.**

> Jeremy Lin is a [1] *basketball player / teacher*. He is from
> [2] *Torrance, California / Harvard University* in the
> United States. His date of birth is August 23, [3] *1988 / 1998*.
> He [4] *speaks / plays* English and Mandarin. He has two
> [5] *sisters / brothers*.

Do you play video games?

☀ CRITICAL THINKING

6 **Work with a partner. Ask and answer the questions.**

UNDERSTAND	APPLY	ANALYZE	EVALUATE
Who is Jeremy's profile for?	What other information do you want to know about Jeremy? Write two questions to ask him.	What information from the text do the pictures show? Do they give other information not in the text?	Does this profile do a good job of showing Jeremy Lin's life? Why or why not?

⚙ COLLABORATION

7 **A** Complete your partner's profile below. Ask the questions and write the answers in the profile.

- What is your name?
- What is your date of birth?
- What country are you from?

- Do you have any brothers or sisters? What are their names?
- What languages do you speak?
- What are your hobbies?

Name	
Date of birth	
Country	
Family	
Languages	
Hobbies	

B Think of two photos that are perfect for your partner's profile. Describe the photos.

C Compare your profiles with another group. Read each person's profile. How are you similar? How are you different?

PREPARING TO READ

1 UNDERSTANDING KEY VOCABULARY **Read the sentences. Write the bold words next to the definitions below.**

1 That is an **unusual** job! I have never heard of it.
2 My brother is a student at an English university. He **lives** in London.
3 My father is a teacher. He **works** in a school.
4 Andrea is **interested in** languages. She wants to learn Japanese.
5 I like to listen to **music**. I like the sound of the piano.
6 I **watch** TV at night. I watch basketball games and other sports.
7 On a **normal** day, I go to work. Then I come home and eat dinner with my family.
8 My **family** is big. I have a mother, a father, four sisters, and three brothers.

a _____ (n) a group of people related to each other, such as a mother, a father, and their children

b _____ (adj) usual, ordinary, and expected

c _____ (v) to have your home somewhere

What do you do on a normal day?

d _____ (adj phr) wanting to learn more about something

e _____ (n) sounds that are made by playing instruments or singing

f _____ (adj) different and not usual; often in a way that is interesting or exciting

g _____ (v) to do a job, especially for money

h _____ (v) to look at something for some time

2 PREVIEWING **You are going to read about an unusual man. Look at the text and photos on pages 24–25. Then circle the correct answers.**

1 The man in the photo on the left is …

    a at a store.   **b** in his home.   **c** in a park.

2 The text is about a …

    a farm.   **b** basketball player.   **c** very tall man.

3 The text is from a …

    a magazine.   **b** newspaper.   **c** web page.

A VERY TALL MAN!

HOW TALL ARE YOU?

1 Sultan Kösen is from Turkey. He **lives** in Mardin in Turkey. He is from a big **family**. He has three brothers and a sister. Sultan also has a wife. His wife is not very tall. She speaks Arabic, and Sultan speaks Turkish and English. They want children in the future.

2 Sultan is a farmer. His hobby is **watching** TV. He is **interested in music**. His height is **unusual**. He is 8 feet 3 inches (251 cm) tall—that is very tall. Sultan is the tallest man in the world. His mother, brothers, and sister are **normal** height.

Sultan Kösen's shoes are size 22.

3 Sultan **works** on a farm. He has a tractor. His life is not easy. People look at him in the street. Normal clothes and shoes are too small. His clothes and shoes are very big.

— " —

"His life is not easy.

4 Sultan likes to travel. Sultan went to London, Paris, and Madrid in Europe in 2010. He went to New York, Chicago, and Los Angeles in the United States in 2011.

Sultan and his wife got married in 2013.

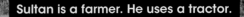

Sultan is a farmer. He uses a tractor.

3 SCANNING TO FIND INFORMATION **Read the text on pages 24–25. Write the correct words from the text in the blanks.**

1 Sultan Kösen _____ from Turkey.

2 He _____ in Mardin in Turkey.

3 He is from a big _____ .

4 Sultan _____ a farmer.

5 His hobby is _____ TV.

6 Sultan _____ Turkish and English.

4 TAKING NOTES **Read the text again and take notes. Write the information in the chart.**

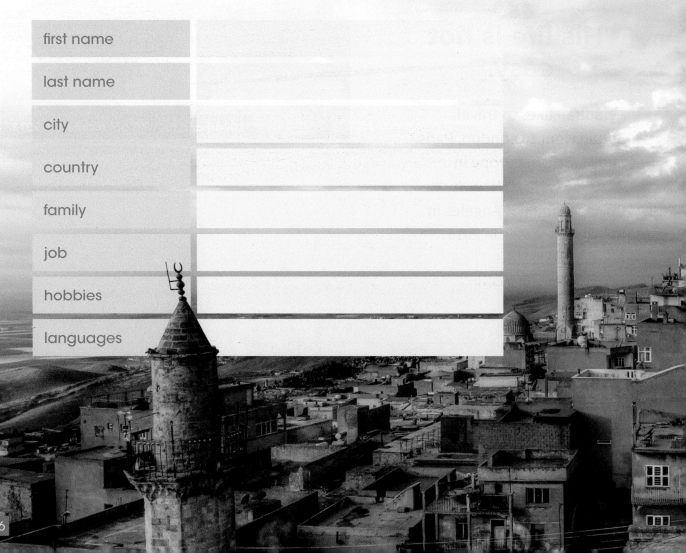

first name	
last name	
city	
country	
family	
job	
hobbies	
languages	

⚙ CRITICAL THINKING

5 SYNTHESIZING **Work with a partner. Use ideas from Reading 1 and Reading 2 to answer the questions.**

UNDERSTAND	APPLY	ANALYZE	EVALUATE
What is Jeremy interested in? What is Sultan interested in?	What can you learn from a profile?	Sultan's life is not easy. Why not?	Do you like reading profiles? Why or why not?

🖧 COLLABORATION

6 **A** Work in a small group. Look at profiles of three famous or interesting people. Ask and answer the questions for each profile.

- What information is in the profile?
- What pictures are in the profile?

B Analyze online profiles. Discuss the questions below with another group. Use the profiles from step A to give examples and explain your ideas.

- Are all profiles interesting?
- What pictures are good for profiles? What pictures are not good?
- What information do people have in their profiles?
- Who looks at profiles?

C Find a profile online, and present it to your group.

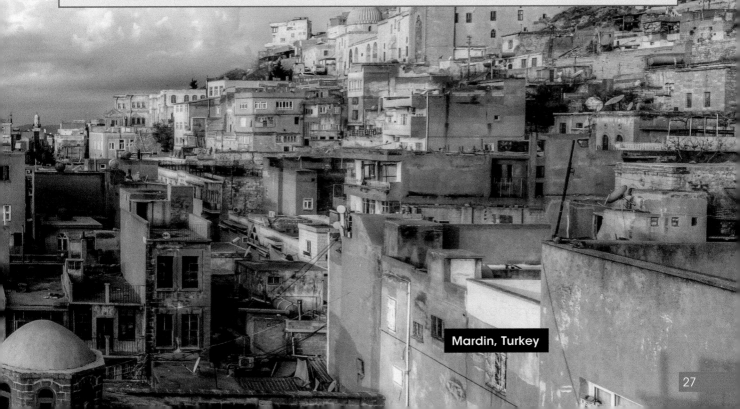

Mardin, Turkey

FAMILY VOCABULARY

1 **Write the nouns from the box in the correct places in the chart below.**

brother   daughter   grandfather   mother   uncle

family vocabulary	
male	**female**
(1) _____	grandmother
father	(4) _____
son	(5) _____
(2) _____	sister
(3) _____	aunt

NOUNS AND VERBS

LANGUAGE

Words for people, places, or things are *nouns*. Words for states or actions are *verbs*. Sentences have nouns and verbs.

nouns: **Sultan** is a **farmer**. He lives in **Mardin**. He works on a **farm**.

verbs: Sultan **is** a farmer. He **lives** in Mardin. He **works** on a farm.

2 **Read the sentences. Write the bold words in the correct columns in the chart on page 29.**

1 Jeremy Lin's mother and father are from **Taiwan**.
2 Sultan Kösen **lives** on a farm.
3 Jeremy Lin's brothers like **basketball**.
4 Sultan Kösen **works** in Turkey.
5 He **is** interested in music.
6 Jeremy Lin **plays** the piano.
7 Sultan speaks two **languages**.

nouns	verbs

SINGULAR AND PLURAL NOUNS

LANGUAGE

Nouns are *singular* or *plural*. Singular means one. Plural means more than one. For most nouns, add -s at the end of the singular form to make the plural form.

singular nouns: Ray has a **brother**. His brother is a **farmer**.

plural nouns: Fernando has two **brothers**. His brothers are **farmers**.

Some plural nouns have irregular forms:

man → **men**   woman → **women**   person → **people**

3 **Read the sentences and circle the correct words.**

1 My mother has four *sister* / *sisters*.
2 I have only one *aunt* / *aunts*.
3 I have a *grandfather* / *grandfathers* in Canada.
4 My grandmother has two *son* / *sons* in the United States.
5 She has five *brother* / *brothers*.

4 **Read the sentences and write the words from the box in the blanks.**

brothers   city   languages   lives   sister   plays

1 Jeremy _____ basketball.

2 Erika is my _____ . She lives with me.

3 She speaks two _____ : Arabic and English.

4 I have a sister and three _____ .

5 My grandfather _____ in Istanbul.

6 Rio de Janeiro is a big _____ . My mother works there.

GLOSSARY

island (n) an area of land that has water around it, like Cuba or Iceland
spend time (v phr) to do something with your time
sail (v) to travel in a boat
dive (v) to jump into water with your head first
equipment (n) the things that you use for a particular activity
goggles (n) special glasses for seeing underwater
easily (adv) with no difficulty

PREPARING TO WATCH

1 ACTIVATING YOUR KNOWLEDGE **Work with a partner and answer the questions.**

1 Where are you from?
2 What do you do in your free time?
3 Imagine you live by the sea. What could you do in your free time?

2 PREDICTING CONTENT USING VISUALS **Look at the pictures from the video. Put the words in order to make sentences.**

1 houses / There are / near the / water / .
2 The boys / a boat / on / are getting / .
3 in / are jumping / The boys / the water / .
4 the sea / in / He / is swimming / .

WHILE WATCHING

▶ **3** UNDERSTANDING MAIN IDEAS **Watch the video. Check (✓) the statements you hear.**

1 ☐ Goon lives by the sea.
2 ☐ The Moken people spend a lot of time in and on the sea.
3 ☐ Goon does not like sailing.
4 ☐ The boys are good swimmers.
5 ☐ The boys need goggles to swim.
6 ☐ They can see everything underwater easily.

4 UNDERSTANDING DETAILS **Watch again. Complete the sentences with the correct words from the box.**

> friends   equipment   jump   family   village

1   His _____ is near the west coast of Thailand.

2   They don't use special _____ or goggles.

3   They _____ from their boat into the water.

4   Goon and his _____ are special.

5   He catches fish and other sea animals for his friends and _____ .

5 MAKING INFERENCES **Circle the correct word.**

1   The Moken people learn to swim when they are *children / adults*.
2   The Moken people eat a lot of *meat / fish*.
3   A *boat / car* is important in the village.
4   The Moken people see easily in the water because *they were born with special eyes / they learn how to see underwater*.

CRITICAL THINKING

6 **Work with a partner and answer the questions.**

APPLY	ANALYZE	EVALUATE
Do you want to live in a village near the sea? Why or why not?	How is Goon's life similar to yours? How is it different?	Which person from this unit has the best life: Jeremy, Sultan, or Goon? Why?

COLLABORATION

7 A Work with a partner. Write a profile for Goon. What two photos can you use for Goon's profile?

B Present your profile to the class, and describe the photos. As a class, vote for the best profile.

CLIMATE

LEARNING OBJECTIVES

Key Reading Skills	Scanning to find information; taking notes in a chart
Additional Reading Skills	Understanding key vocabulary; using your knowledge; previewing; reading for details; synthesizing
Language Development	Nouns and adjectives; noun phrases

ACTIVATE YOUR KNOWLEDGE

Work with a partner. Look at the photo and discuss the questions.

1   Does this look like a nice time of year? Why or why not?
2   Does this look like your country? Why or why not?
3   What time of year do you like best? Why?

PREPARING TO READ

1 UNDERSTANDING KEY VOCABULARY **You are going to read an article about a city with cold weather. Work with a partner. Read the sentences, and look at the words in bold. Use the words to describe the photos.**

1 Florida is **warm**. In the **summer**, everyone enjoys the sun.
2 Canada is **cold**. In the **winter**, the temperatures are freezing.
3 **Spring** is before **summer**. **Fall** is before **winter**.

2 USING YOUR KNOWLEDGE **Match the words to the correct numbers.**

1 eleven   a 8
2 eighteen   b 18
3 twenty-one   c 6
4 forty-two   d 42
5 fifty   e 21
6 eight   f 11
7 six   g 50

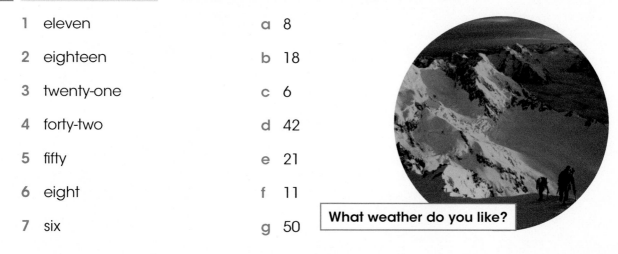

What weather do you like?

3 USING YOUR KNOWLEDGE **Look at the temperatures. Work with a partner and discuss the questions.**

> 30° F (−1° C) 60° F (16° C) 80° F (27° C)

1   Which temperature do you like best? Why?
2   What do people do outside for each temperature?
3   What are the temperatures where you live?

4 PREVIEWING **Look at the graph, photographs, and headings in the text on pages 36–37. Write *T* (true) or *F* (false) next to the statements.**

_____   1   Yakutsk is a city.

_____   2   Winter is very cold in Yakutsk.

_____   3   Summer is very cold in Yakutsk.

_____   4   Svetlana has a café in Moscow.

What temperature is it?

THE COLDEST
CITY IN THE
WORLD

WHAT COLD CITIES HAVE YOU VISITED?

by MIKAELA MORRIS

> "
> **I wanted to meet the people of Yakutsk.**

1 The temperature in your freezer is **cold**. It is about 0° F (−18° C). The city of Yakutsk in Russia is colder than your freezer. In the **winter**, the average temperature is −44° F (−42° C)!

2 In 2016, I visited Yakutsk. Why? Because I wanted to see the coldest city in the world. I wanted to meet the people of Yakutsk.

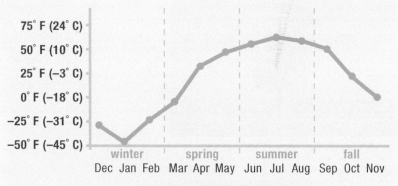

Average temperatures in Yakutsk
(December – November)

3 "Life is difficult in the winter," says Svetlana, "but we're not sad." Svetlana is the manager of a café[1] in Yakutsk. She has two children. Her son Pavel is 11. Her daughter Daria is 5.

4 "The average temperature in the winter is –44° F (–42° C). Some winters are colder. At –40° F (–40° C), the kindergarten[2] is closed. Daria is happy. At –49° F (–45° C), the kindergarten and the school are closed. Daria and Pavel are happy," Svetlana says.

> **" Winters are the coldest in the world here.**

5 People in Yakutsk like sports[3]. In the **spring** and **fall**, the average temperature is –6° F (–21° C). They go skiing and ice skating. In the **summer**, it is **warm**. The average temperature is 68° F (20° C). People take food and drinks to eat outside.

[1]café (n) a small restaurant where you can buy drinks and food

[2]kindergarten (n) a class for young children, usually four or five years old

[3]sports (n) games or activities that people do to keep healthy or for fun

People ice skate and ski in the spring and fall in Yakutsk.

Svetlana has a warm café in a cold city.

It was cold, but fun!

SCANNING TO FIND INFORMATION

Scanning means looking for information. When we scan, we do not read every word in a text. We can scan for:

- numbers
- names of people
- names of places

Look for capital letters to find people and places.

5 SCANNING TO FIND INFORMATION **Scan the text on pages 36–37. Match the facts to the correct numbers.**

1	the average temperature in the summer	a	–44° F (–42° C)
2	the year the writer went to Yakutsk	b	2016
3	the average temperature in the winter	c	5
4	Daria's age	d	–49° F (–45° C)
5	the average temperature in spring and fall	e	–6° F (–21° C)
6	the temperature when kindergartens and schools are closed	f	68° F (20° C)

6 READING FOR DETAILS **Read the text. Write the words from the box in the blanks to summarize the text.**

cold   spring   Svetlana   warm   Yakutsk

The text is about (1) _____ and her family. They live in the city of

(2) _____ in Russia. The winters are very (3) _____ .

Sometimes school is closed. In the (4) _____ and fall, people go skiing

and ice skating. In the summer, it is (5) _____ .

🔆 CRITICAL THINKING

7 **Work with a partner and answer the questions.**

UNDERSTAND	APPLY	ANALYZE	EVALUATE
How hot is the summer in your country?	What do you do in cold temperatures?	When is the best time to visit Yakutsk? Why?	Do you want to live in Yakutsk? Why or why not?

🐾 COLLABORATION

8 **A** Work with a partner. Choose a town or city with very warm weather. Find answers to the questions.

- Where is the city?

- What is the average temperature?

- What is the warmest temperature?

- How long is the summer? How long is the winter?

- What do people do in the summer? What do people do in the winter?

B Share your information with the class. As a class, rank the cities or towns from warmest to coldest.

READING 2

PREPARING TO READ

1 USING YOUR KNOWLEDGE **Work with a partner. Talk about the winter, spring, summer, and fall in your city or town. Do you have all four seasons? What months are in each season?**

MONTHS					
January	February	March	April	May	June
July	August	September	October	November	December

2 **Match each photo with a word in bold.**

1 It's very **rainy**. Let's stay inside. _____

2 It's a **sunny** day! Let's go to the beach. _____

3 It's **cloudy**. I can't see the sun. _____

4 It's so **windy**! I lost my hat. _____

3 UNDERSTANDING KEY VOCABULARY **You are going to read about the climate in Cuba. Read the definitions. Then write the words from the box in the blanks.**

> **dry** (adj) with very little or no rain
> **rainfall** (n) the amount of rain that falls in one place
> **season** (n) one of the four periods of the year: winter, spring, summer, or fall
> **climate** (n) the weather that an area usually has

1   The _____ in spring is often high. It is good for the plants.

2   Summer is my favorite _____ . I like warm temperatures.

3   The desert is very _____ . Little rain falls there.

4   The _____ in the desert is hot and dry.

4 PREVIEWING **Look at Parts A, B, and C on pages 42–43. Circle the correct answers to the questions.**

1   Where is the text from?

   a a book   b a magazine   c a web page

2   Which part is about the weather in Cuba now?

   a Part A   b Part B   c Part C

3   Which parts are about normal weather in Cuba?

   a Parts A and B   b Parts B and C   c Parts A and C

CUBA WEATHER

SIGN IN

(A)

1   Cuba is in the Caribbean. The **climate** in Cuba is good. It has two **seasons**: the **dry** season and the **rainy** season. The dry season and the rainy season each last for six months.

2   The dry season is from November to April. The average temperatures are between 72° F (22° C) and 77° F (25° C) in the dry season. The average **rainfall** is 2.6 inches (62 mm) in the dry season. It is **windy** and **sunny** in the dry season.

3   The rainy season is from May to October. In the rainy season, the average temperatures are between 79° F (26° C) and 82° F (28° C). The average rainfall in the rainy season is 5.7 inches (146 mm). It is often **cloudy**.

4   The best month to visit Cuba is April or May.

B   TODAY   TOMORROW   5 DAY   MONTHLY

Today	Monday	Tuesday	Wednesday	Thursday
84° F (29° C)	82° F (28° C)	79° F (26° C)	84° F (29° C)	88° F (31° C)
cloudy	rainy	sunny	windy	sunny

C   TODAY   TOMORROW   5 DAY   MONTHLY

Season (months)	Average temperature	Average rainfall	Average wind speed
Dry (Nov.–Apr.)	73° F (23° C)	2.6 inches (62 mm)	5 mph (8 kph)
Rainy (May–Oct.)	81° F (27° C)	5.7 inches (146 mm)	9 mph (15 kph)

5 SCANNING TO FIND INFORMATION **Scan the text on pages 42–43. Match the facts to the correct numbers.**

1	number of months in the dry season	a	79
2	average temperature (°F) in the dry season	b	88
3	average rainfall (inches) in the dry season	c	73
4	average rainfall (inches) in the rainy season	d	5.7
5	temperature (°F) on Tuesday	e	6
6	temperature (°F) on Thursday	f	2.6

🔧 SKILLS

TAKING NOTES IN A CHART

A chart shows facts and numbers. Use a chart to take notes on important facts and numbers in a reading

season	months	weather
spring	March, April, May	average temperature: −6° F (−21° C); cold weather

---

6 TAKING NOTES **Read the text. Use the chart to take notes about the weather in Cuba.**

season	months	weather

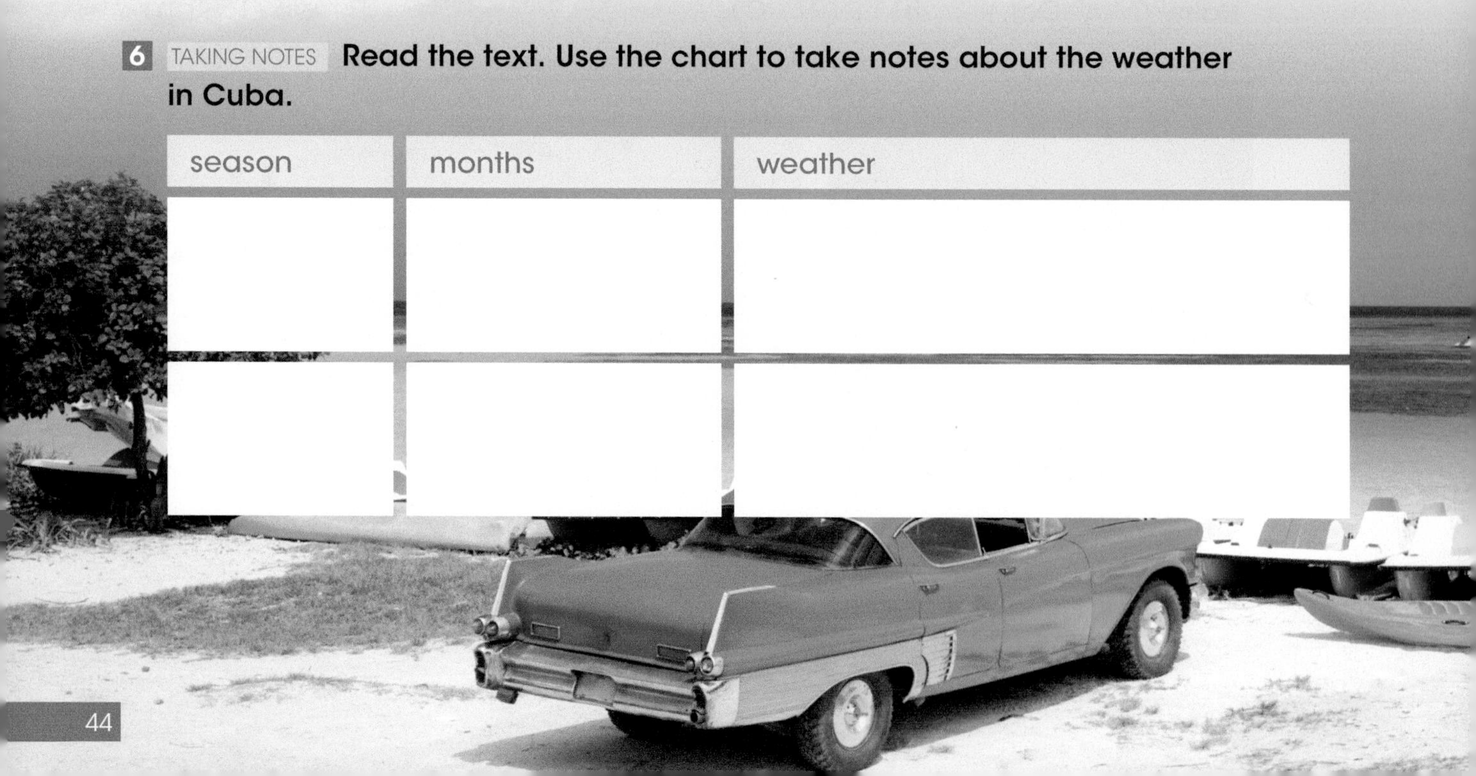

☼ CRITICAL THINKING

7 SYNTHESIZING **Work with a partner. Use ideas from Reading 1 and Reading 2 to answer the questions.**

UNDERSTAND	APPLY	ANALYZE	EVALUATE
What are the seasons in Cuba?	When is a good time to visit Cuba? Why do you think those months are good?	Where can you find facts about the climate in a country?	Why do people want to know about the weather and climate of a place?

⚙ COLLABORATION

8 **A** Work with a small group. Choose a city or town, and record the weather this week in the chart. Draw a picture or icon for the weather each day.

Monday	Tuesday	Wednesday	Thursday	Friday

B Take turns. Report the weather for each day to the rest of the class.

NOUNS AND ADJECTIVES

> **LANGUAGE**
>
> Words for people, places, or things are *nouns*. Words that describe people, places, and things are *adjectives*. Adjectives can come after the verb *be*. They describe the subject.
>
> The <u>winter</u> is **cold**. The <u>climate</u> is **good**.
>
> <u>August</u> is **hot**. It is **cloudy**. It is **sunny**.

1 **Underline the nouns and circle the adjectives in the sentences.**

1 The café is warm.
2 October is rainy.
3 The climate is good.
4 Summers are hot.
5 Winters are cold.

2 **Read the sentences. Write the adjectives from the box in the blanks.**

> cloudy   cold   difficult   happy   sunny

1 In Yakutsk, life is _____ in the winter.

2 The children are _____ .

3 It is warm and _____ today.

4 The winter is _____ in Yakutsk.

5 The rainy season is _____ .

NOUN PHRASES

LANGUAGE

A *noun phrase* is a noun and another word that describes or defines the noun. When an adjective comes before a noun, it is part of a noun phrase.

Cuba has **a good climate**. Cuba has **a dry season**.

The average rainfall is 2.6 inches. **The rainy season** is from May to October.

3 Make a noun phrase from the bold words in each sentence. Write it in the blanks to make a new sentence.

1 Yakutsk's **winters** are **cold**.

Yakutsk has _____ _____ .

2 The **season** is **dry** from November to April.

The _____ _____ is from November to April.

3 In the rainy season, the **rainfall** is **high**.

The rainy season has _____ _____ .

4 **Summers** are **warm** in Yakutsk.

Yakutsk has _____ _____ .

4 Work with a partner. Correct the mistakes in the sentences. Look for mistakes in noun phrases or adjectives after the verb *be*.

1 Cuba has a season rainy.

_____

2 Yakutsk has a fall cold.

_____

3 In the summer, we have weather sunny.

_____

4 The dry season windy is.

_____

5 In spring, the rainfall high is.

_____

GLOSSARY

river (n) a long natural area of water that flows across the land

fir trees / pine trees (n) trees with thin, hard green leaves that stay green all winter

forest (n) a large area with many trees growing closely together

freezing / frozen (adj) very cold; turned into ice

heavy snow (n phr) a lot of snow

PREPARING TO WATCH

1 ACTIVATING YOUR KNOWLEDGE **Work with a partner and answer the questions.**

1 Which seasons do you have in your country?

2 Do you prefer hot and sunny weather or cold and snowy weather? Why?

3 Where in the world is it very cold?

2 PREDICTING CONTENT USING VISUALS **Look at the pictures from the video. Write _T_ (true) or _F_ (false) next to the statements.**

____ 1 This part of the Earth is warm.

____ 2 Part of the river is frozen.

____ 3 There is ice and snow on the trees.

____ 4 The trees die in the winter.

WHILE WATCHING

▶ **3** UNDERSTANDING MAIN IDEAS **Watch the video. Check (✓) the statements you hear.**

1 ☐ The days grow short and cold.

2 ☐ Winter is hard here.

3 ☐ Water in the air, in rivers, and in plants turns to ice.

4 ☐ All of the plants die.

5 ☐ Heavy snow covers the taiga.

6 ☐ Cold temperatures return in the spring.

(▶) **4** UNDERSTANDING DETAILS **Watch again. Circle the correct answer.**

1 Snow and cold temperatures move *north* / *south*.

2 Fir trees can live in very *warm* / *cold* temperatures.

3 The taiga forest has almost *20%* / *30%* of all the trees on Earth.

4 Heavy *snow* / *rain* covers part of the taiga until the spring.

5 MAKING INFERENCES **Complete the sentences with the words from the box.**

> difficult   flowers   near   winter

1 The _____ is very long in the taiga forest.

2 The taiga forest is _____ the North Pole.

3 Living in the taiga forest is _____ in the winter.

4 _____ do not grow in the winter in the taiga forest.

☼ CRITICAL THINKING

6 Work with a partner and answer the questions.

UNDERSTAND	APPLY	EVALUATE
Is it easy for people to live in the taiga forest? Why or why not?	Which season is the longest in your country?	Which place do you want to visit: Yakutsk, Cuba, or the taiga? Why?

⚇ COLLABORATION

7 A Work in a small group. Choose a city or town, and complete the chart.

City or town: _____

Season	Months	Weather	Things to do

B Write a blog post with the information from your chart. Add a title and photos to your post. Share the blog with your class. As a class, vote for the city or town with the best climate.

LIFESTYLE

LEARNING OBJECTIVES

Key Reading Skill	Annotating
Additional Reading Skills	Understanding key vocabulary; using your knowledge; predicting content using visuals; scanning to find information; reading for main ideas; previewing; reading for details; synthesizing
Language Development	Collocations for free-time activities; time expressions

ACTIVATE YOUR KNOWLEDGE

1 **Look at the photo and ask and answer the questions with a partner. Use the names of places from the box to help you.**

> café   home   park

1 Where are the people?
2 What are they doing?
3 What do you do in the evening?
4 Where do you go with friends for fun? Why?

PREPARING TO READ

1 UNDERSTANDING KEY VOCABULARY **Read the sentences and write each bold word next to the correct definition.**

1 I do not like to wake up early. I **get up** around 10:00 a.m.

2 I like to **cook** my food at home, but many of my friends eat at restaurants.

3 Before I go to work, I have coffee and toast for **breakfast** every morning.

4 I usually eat **lunch** at my desk at work. I usually have a salad or soup.

5 I eat **dinner** after work. Sometimes, I eat with friends at a restaurant.

6 I often **travel** to China and Japan for my work.

7 I **meet** a lot of people in my job. I really enjoy talking with new people.

8 I **swim** every Saturday. I take lessons at a pool near my house.

a _____ (n) the food you eat at the end of the day

b _____ (phr v) to rise from bed after sleeping

c _____ (v) to see and speak to someone for the first time

d _____ (n) the food you eat in the morning after you wake up

e _____ (v) to move through water by moving your body

f _____ (v) to prepare food by heating it

g _____ (n) the food you eat in the middle of the day

h _____ (v) to go from one place to another, usually over a long distance

2 USING YOUR KNOWLEDGE **You are going to read about a book that shows a different way of life. Ask and answer the questions with a partner.**

1　Imagine you do not have a smartphone or TV. What do you do? How do you spend your time?

2　Imagine there are no supermarkets or restaurants. What do you eat? Where do you get food?

3 PREDICTING CONTENT USING VISUALS **Which things in the box can you see in the photos on pages 54–55? Circle the words. Use a dictionary to help you.**

| a writer　a hunter　a jungle　a tree house　a TV　a website　a watch |

Do you swim?

MEET THE KOMBAI

Can you imagine your life with no smartphones or TV? With no cars or supermarkets? Can you imagine life in a tree house?

1 In her book, *A Life in the Trees*, journalist[1] Rebecca Moore **travels** 9,321 miles (15,000 km) from London to Papua on the island of New Guinea. In Papua, Rebecca **meets** the Kombai people. She writes about their lives in the jungle.

2 Moore lived with the Kombai women and children for three months. Kombai life is very different. The Kombai people have no watches[2] and no cars. There is no school for the children. Parents[3] teach their children to **cook**, hunt, and **swim**.

Kombai tree house

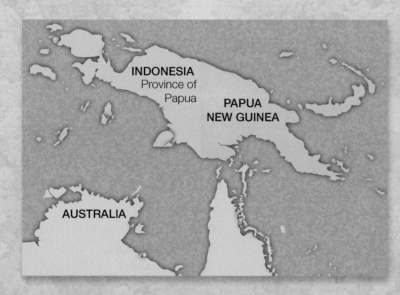

INDONESIA
Province of Papua

PAPUA
NEW GUINEA

AUSTRALIA

"It has amazing photographs on every page."
Simon Higgins, *New Look*

"Buy this book!"
Jeffrey Rost, *Lifestyle*

The Kombai men can hunt for 12 hours a day.

Kombai women prepare the sago palms.

3 The Kombai **get up** every morning at sunrise. Kombai men hunt in the jungle. They can hunt for 12 hours. They also cut down sago palms. This tree is important. The women cook the inside of the tree. The Kombai people eat this food for **breakfast**, **lunch**, and **dinner**.

4 The most important part of Kombai life is building their tree houses. The men, women, and children all help build tree houses. Each house is 66 feet (20 m) high. The stories in this book show the Kombai people's lives in the trees.

¹journalist (n) someone whose job is writing for newspapers

²watches (n) small clocks on a strap that you wear around your wrist

³parents (n) mother and father

WHILE READING

4 SCANNING TO FIND INFORMATION **Read the text on pages 54–55, and check (✓) the person or people who do each action. There may be more than one answer.**

		Rebecca Moore	Kombai men	Kombai women	Kombai children
1	hunt in the jungle		✓		
2	travels 9,321 miles (15,000 km)				
3	cook sago palms				
4	eat sago palms				
5	have no cars				
6	teach children to hunt, cook, and swim				
7	build tree houses				
8	tells the story of the Kombai way of life				

5 READING FOR MAIN IDEAS **Match the sentence halves to create complete sentences.**

1   In Papua, Rebecca meets   a   the sago palm.

2   The Kombai women cook   b   the Kombai people.

3   The Kombai people have   c   build tree houses.

4   The men, women, and children help   d   a different life.

6 **Read the text again to check your answers in Exercise 5.**

⚡ CRITICAL THINKING

7 **Work with a partner. Ask and answer the questions.**

UNDERSTAND	APPLY	ANALYZE
What do the Kombai people teach their children? Why?	Why do you think the Kombai live in tree houses?	What do you learn from your family? Why?

🐾 COLLABORATION

A   Work in groups of four. Prepare five interview questions for the Kombai people about their lives. Use the information from Reading 1 to help you.

1   _____

2   _____

3   _____

4   _____

5   _____

B   Role-play the interview. Each person in your group will be one of the following people:

• Rebecca Moore (the interviewer)   • a Kombai woman

• a Kombai man   • a Kombai child

Ask and answer the questions in your group. Then do the role play in front of the class.

READING 2

1 UNDERSTANDING KEY VOCABULARY **You are going to read about a college student's daily schedule. Read the sentences. Choose the best definition for the words in bold.**

1 After lunch, I like to take a nap in the **afternoon**.
   a a time between 12 p.m. and 5 p.m.
   b something you eat for lunch

2 I am very **busy** with school. I take many classes.
   a having a lot of friends
   b having a lot of things to do

3 My **schedule** is the same every day. I work and then go to school.
   a a place where you work to make money
   b a list of planned activities or things that need to be done

4 I get up at 6 a.m. every **morning**. I make coffee and eat breakfast.
   a a time between 5 a.m. and 12 p.m.
   b the place where you make food

5 I **relax** after work. I watch TV.
   a to become calm and comfortable
   b to have many things to do

6 In the **evening**, I do my homework and read a book before bed.
   a a place you go to relax
   b a time between 5 p.m. and 11 p.m.

7 I have school on **weekdays**. I have to get up early.
   a Monday to Friday, when many people work
   b Saturday and Sunday, when many people do not work

8 On the **weekend**, I ride my bike. I have fun with friends.
   a Saturday and Sunday, when many people do not work
   b Monday to Friday, when many people work

2 Write the bold words from Exercise 1 in the correct places in the chart. Some words go in more than one place.

noun	verb	adjective	part of the day	part of the week

3 USING YOUR KNOWLEDGE **List things you do on weekdays and on the weekend. Compare your list with a partner.**

weekdays	weekend
Monday, Tuesday, Wednesday, Thursday, Friday	Saturday and Sunday

4 PREVIEWING **Look at Reading 2 on pages 60–61. Write *T* (true) or *F* (false) next to the statements. After you read the text, check your answers.**

_____ 1 The schedule is for an engineering student.

_____ 2 The schedule and the text are from a website.

_____ 3 The text and the schedule are about Matteo Taha.

Name of student: Matteo Taha   **Major:** Engineering

morning							
	Sun.	Mon.	Tue.	Wed.	Thur.	Fri.	Sat.
8–9 a.m.		Physics 101	Physics 101	Physics 101	Physics 101	Physics 101	
9:15–10:15 a.m.		Calculus 121	Calculus 121	Calculus 121	Calculus 121	Calculus 121	
10:30–11:30 a.m.		Engineering 122	Engineering 122	Engineering 122	Engineering 122	Engineering 122	
afternoon							
	Sun.	Mon.	Tue.	Wed.	Thur.	Fri.	Sat.
12:30–1:30 p.m.						Study group	
2–3 p.m.		English 101	History 204	English 101	History 204		
evening							
	Sun.	Mon.	Tue.	Wed.	Thur.	Fri.	Sat.
5–7 p.m.	Relax with friends	Library	Library	Library		Library	
7–10 p.m.	Relax with friends	Library		Go to the gym		Library	

To Alexandra Roobio

From Mark Holand

Subject Matteo Taha

Hi Alexandra,

1 Thank you for your email. I'm happy to tell you about Matteo. Matteo Taha is a new student. He has a **busy schedule**. Matteo studies engineering[1] here at the University of Michigan. He takes five classes. They are physics[2], calculus[3], English, engineering, and history[4]. His favorite classes are physics and calculus.

2 Matteo has three classes every **weekday morning**. He gets up at 6 a.m. every day. Then he has physics from 8 a.m. to 9 a.m., calculus from 9:15 a.m. to 10:15 a.m., and engineering from 10:30 a.m. to 11:30 a.m.

3 On Monday and Wednesday **afternoons**, he has English. His English class is from 2 p.m. to 3 p.m. On Tuesday and Thursday afternoons, he has history from 2 p.m. to 3 p.m. On Friday afternoons, he meets with his study group. His study group is from 12:30 p.m. to 1:30 p.m. In the **evenings**, Matteo often studies in the library.

4 On the **weekends**, Matteo **relaxes** with friends. Sometimes, he goes to the pool to swim. He enjoys his busy life.

5 Matteo is doing well, but please let me know if you have any more questions.

Sincerely,

Mark Holand

[1]engineering (n) the study of designing and building buildings, bridges, roads, etc.

[2]physics (n) the study of natural forces, such as energy, heat, light, etc.

[3]calculus (n) the study of a high level of math

[4]history (n) the study of past events

ANNOTATING

When you *annotate*, you mark the text. For example, you can underline key words. Key words are the words or phrases that give the important information in the text. Look at the underlined words in the paragraph below. The reader has underlined the key words that give the most important information and details.

> In her book, *A Life in the Trees*, journalist <u>Rebecca Moore</u> travels 9,321 miles (15,000 km) from London to Papua on the island of New Guinea. In Papua, Rebecca <u>meets the Kombai people</u>. She writes about their <u>lives</u> <u>in the jungle</u>.

5 ANNOTATING **Read the schedule and email on pages 60–61. Underline two to three key words or phrases in each paragraph of the email. Then compare your key words with a partner. What is the important information?**

6 READING FOR DETAILS **Use the text and your key words. Circle the correct word to make true sentences.**

1 Matteo has a busy *class* / *schedule*.
2 He is a *teacher* / *student* at the University of Michigan.
3 He takes five *classes* / *weekdays*.
4 He has three classes every weekday *morning* / *afternoon*.
5 He *relaxes* / *studies* on the weekends.

☼ CRITICAL THINKING

7 SYNTHESIZING **Work with a partner. Use ideas from Reading 1 and Reading 2 to answer the questions.**

UNDERSTAND

When does Matteo relax? What does he do to relax?

APPLY

When do you relax? What do you do to relax?

ANALYZE

Compare your life to the Kombai people and to Matteo. What is similar? What is different?

☼ COLLABORATION

8 **A** Work with a partner. Interview your partner and complete the schedule. Write the activities and times in the schedule.

When do you get up? What classes do you take? What time are your classes?

Name of student: _____ **Major:** _____

	Sun.	Mon.	Tue.	Wed.	Thur.	Fri.	Sat.
Morning							
Afternoon							
Evening							

B Change partners. Ask questions and compare schedules. Find three things that are the same and three things that are different.

C Repeat step B.

LANGUAGE DEVELOPMENT

COLLOCATIONS FOR FREE-TIME ACTIVITIES

LANGUAGE

A pair or small group of words that are often used together is a *collocation*. One type of collocation is **a verb** + **a noun** or **a noun phrase**.

sentence	collocation
I **have breakfast**.	have + breakfast
They **play video games.**	play + video games
Matteo **studies English**.	studies + English

Another type of collocation is **a verb** + **a prepositional phrase**.

sentence	collocation
Matteo **goes to the gym**.	goes + to the gym
Matteo **studies in the library**.	studies + in the library
Matteo **relaxes with friends**.	relaxes + with friends

1 **Match the sentence halves.**

1	Fernando **studies**	a	**coffee** before work.
2	Matteo **gets up**	b	**physics** at Yale University.
3	Melody and Ginger **take**	c	**at 6 a.m.**
4	In the morning, **I have**	d	**to the gym** every Saturday.
5	My friends **go**	e	**the bus** every morning.

2 **Read the sentences and write the verbs from the box in the blanks.**

> do   eats   go   have   meets   take

1   Matteo _____ **with** his study group on Fridays.

2   I _____ **a shower** before breakfast every morning.

3 You _____ **to the gym** every day.

4 Melody and Ginger _____ **breakfast** at 7 a.m!

5 Li Mei _____ **her lunch** in the café.

6 You _____ **your homework** in the evening.

TIME EXPRESSIONS

LANGUAGE

Time expressions say **when** or **how often** something happens. One type of time expression is *every* + a noun.

I do my homework **every week**. They swim **every morning**.

Another type of time expression is a prepositional phrase for time. The preposition depends on the noun phrase that follows.

* *at* + clock time: **at** 10 a.m., **at** 3 p.m.
* *in* + part of the day: **in** the morning, **in** the afternoon, **in** the evening
* *on* + day of the week: **on** Monday, **on** Tuesdays
* *on* + day of the week + part of the day: **on** Monday morning, **on** Tuesday afternoon, **on** Friday evening, **on** Sunday night

3 Write *at*, *in*, or *on* in the blanks.

1 Simon swims _____ Saturday morning _____ 8 a.m.

2 _____ the evening, Matteo studies in the library.

3 _____ Monday, I have English class _____ 2 p.m.

4 I talk to my family _____ the evening.

5 _____ Tuesday morning, David has calculus _____ 11 a.m.

6 Paulo goes to the university _____ Monday and Thursday.

7 I do my homework _____ the afternoon.

8 Andrea goes to work _____ 7 a.m. every weekday.

WATCH AND LISTEN

 1    2   3    4

GLOSSARY

coast (n) the land next to the ocean

deep (adj) having a long distance from top to bottom, like the middle of the ocean

culture (n) the habits and traditions of a country or group of people

sweep (v) to clean, especially a floor, by using a broom or brush

raise (v) to take care of from a young age

PREPARING TO WATCH

1   ACTIVATING YOUR KNOWLEDGE   **Work with a partner and answer the questions.**

1   What are five things that you do every day?

2   What jobs do people in the mountains do? What do you think they do every day?

3   What jobs do people on islands do? What do you think they do every day?

4   What do you think is better, living in the mountains or living on an island? Why?

2   PREDICTING CONTENT USING VISUALS   **Match the sentences to the pictures (1–4) from the video.**

a   The women wear colorful clothes. _____

b   The people grow plants. _____

c   There is a village on the island. _____

d   The man is catching food to eat. _____

WHILE WATCHING

▶ **3**   UNDERSTANDING MAIN IDEAS   **Watch the video. Check (✓) the statements you hear.**

1   ☐   The Kuna people live in Venezuela.

2   ☐   Many of the Kuna are fishermen.

3   ☐   They work on big farms.

4   ☐   Music is important to Kuna men, women, and children.

▶ **4** UNDERSTANDING DETAILS **Watch again. Write *T* (true) or *F* (false) next to the statements. Correct the false statements.**

_____ 1 About 35,000 Kuna men, women, and children live on islands near the coast of Colombia.

_____ 2 Kuna fishermen swim more than 200 feet deep.

_____ 3 They wear colorful clothes every day.

_____ 4 They have large gardens around their homes.

_____ 5 In their free time, they fish.

5 MAKING INFERENCES **Complete the sentences with the words or phrases in the box. You will not use all the words.**

colorful   clothing   fish   land   long
meat   music and dancing   short   swimming

1 The Kuna people have lived on the islands for a _____ time.

2 They often eat _____ .

3 They celebrate with _____ .

4 The Kuna people love and care for their _____ .

💡 CRITICAL THINKING

6 Work with a partner and answer the questions.

UNDERSTAND	ANALYZE	ANALYZE
What do you like about the Kuna people's lifestyle?	What do you think is difficult about their lifestyle? Why?	How is their lifestyle different from yours?

COLLABORATION

7 A Think about the lifestyles and cultures of the people in this unit: the Kombai people in Papua, a college student in the United States, and the Kuna people in Central America. Which culture do you want to live in?

B Work with a partner. Describe the culture, what you like about it, and why.

C Share your ideas with the class. Describe a normal day in the life you choose.

PLACES

ACTIVATE YOUR KNOWLEDGE

Work with a partner. Ask and answer the questions.

1 What place is in the picture?

2 Why do people go there?

3 Do you want to visit this place? Why or why not?

4 What places do people visit in your country?

The Nile River Valley in Egypt

PREPARING TO READ

1 UNDERSTANDING KEY VOCABULARY **Read the sentences. Choose the best definition for the word or phrase in bold.**

1   The Great Lakes in North America are very big, but the **lake** by my house is small.
   a   salt water that covers most of the Earth
   b   an area of fresh water that has land all around it

2   Lakes have fresh water, but **seas**, like the Mediterranean, have salt water.
   a   a large area of very dry land
   b   large areas of salt water

3   I do not like to climb **mountains**. I do not like to be up high.
   a   very high hills
   b   land that is low, near the water

4   There are many trees in a **forest**. They are homes for birds and other animals.
   a   a large area of salt water
   b   a large area of trees growing closely together

5   The Nile is the longest **river** in the world. It is 4,258 miles (6,853 km) long.
   a   water that flows across the land to a bigger area of water
   b   a large area of land with many trees

6   There are five **oceans**. These are the biggest bodies of water in the world.
   a   one of the five main areas of salt water on the Earth
   b   an area of sand or rocks next to water

7   People use **maps** to help them find places and understand an area.
   a   pictures that show a place and the rivers, lakes, and other areas in it
   b   boats, cars, and other things that people drive

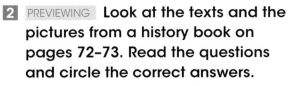

2 PREVIEWING **Look at the texts and the pictures from a history book on pages 72–73. Read the questions and circle the correct answers.**

1   What is the book about?

   a   the history of the world

   b   the history of China

   c   the history of maps

2   What is the first chapter of the book?

   a   Discovering America

   b   First maps of the world

   c   Table of contents

3   What does the picture at the top of page 73 show?

   a   a modern map of the world

   b   an old map of the world

   c   a photograph of the world

When do you use maps?

TAKE A LOOK!

Feedback | Help | Close

A World History of Maps

by J.T. Kirk

Add to Basket

Price: from $16.75

Table of contents

2.2 Muhammad al-Idrisi's World Map

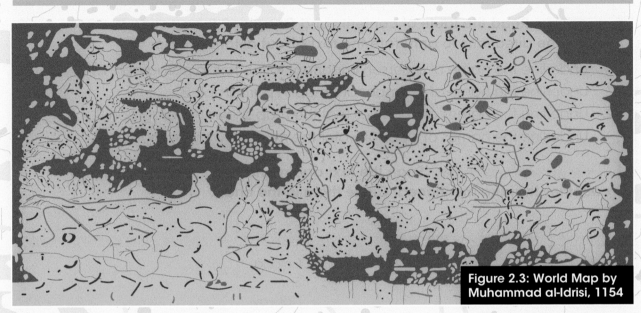

Figure 2.3: World Map by Muhammad al-Idrisi, 1154

1 Muhammad al-Idrisi came from Morocco. He studied in North Africa and Spain. As a young man, he traveled in Spain, North Africa, France, England, and parts of Asia. In 1145, he began working for King Roger II of Sicily. Al-Idrisi created his **map** of the world then.

2 Al-Idrisi's map of the world is called the *Tabula Rogeriana* in Europe. The map is in Arabic. Al-Idrisi used information from earlier Arabic and Greek maps. He also used information from explorers. These men were sent to the different countries to draw and record what they saw. This map helped people travel from country to country.

3 The map shows North Africa, Europe, and South and East Asia. There are many European countries on the map. There is Norway in the north, Spain in the west, and Italy in the south. The map also shows India and China.

Muhammed al-Idrisi

4 There are **forests, rivers, lakes, mountains, seas,** and **oceans** on the map. Al-Idrisi's map shows the Mediterranean Sea, the Indian Ocean, and the Nile River.

3 ANNOTATING **Read the table of contents and Chapter 2.2 on pages 72–73. Follow the directions to annotate the text about al-Idrisi's map.**

1 Underline the name of a person important to the text in paragraph 1.
2 Underline the name of an important map in paragraph 2.
3 Underline the names of countries that the map shows in paragraph 3.
4 Underline the names of types of water the map shows in paragraph 4.

4 SCANNING TO FIND INFORMATION **Scan the text again and find the continents and countries that are mentioned. Circle them in the chart.**

continents	countries
Asia	Finland
Australia	Spain
Europe	Norway
Africa	Canada
North America	Morocco
South America	China
Antarctica	The United States

5 READING FOR DETAILS **Read Chapter 2.2 on pages 72–73. Write *T* (true) or *F* (false) next to the statements. Correct the false statements.**

_____ 1 Muhammad al-Idrisi was Algerian.

_____ 2 The *Tabula Rogeriana* is written in Greek.

_____ 3 South America is not on the map.

_____ 4 India is on the map.

_____ 5 There are lakes on the map.

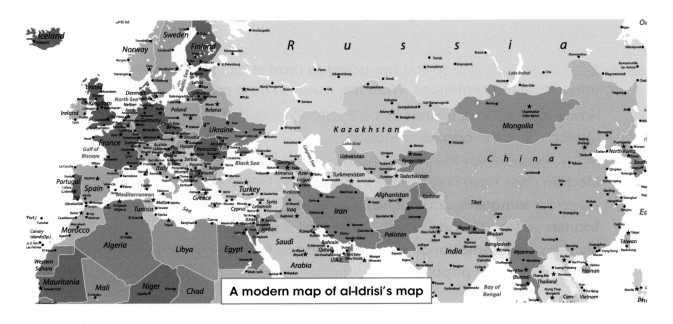

A modern map of al-Idrisi's map

☼ CRITICAL THINKING

6 **Work with a partner. Answer the questions.**

REMEMBER	APPLY	ANALYZE
How did al-Idrisi make his map?	What can you learn from a very old map?	How do you think maps are different today?

☷ COLLABORATION

7 **A** Work with a partner from your country if possible. Draw a map of your country. Add important mountains, lakes, seas, rivers, forests, and cities.

B Compare your map with a real map. Answer the questions.

• What details are correct? Why did you remember this information?

• What details are not correct? Why were they difficult to remember?

C Change partners. Sit back to back. Take turns describing your map to your partner. Your partner draws the map on a piece of paper and asks questions for clarification.

D When you finish step C, compare your maps. Discuss what is correct and incorrect.

PREPARING TO READ

1 UNDERSTANDING KEY VOCABULARY **You are going to read a fact file about an island country. Read the sentences. Write the words in bold next to the definitions.**

1 Hawaii is a group of **islands** in the Pacific Ocean.
2 Mexico City is the **capital** of Mexico.
3 Many people enjoy the water and sun at the **beach**.
4 **Modern** cities have new buildings, parks, and businesses.
5 Arizona is **famous** because it has the Grand Canyon. Many people visit there.
6 **Tourists** visit the Grand Canyon because it is a beautiful place.
7 My school is **international**. There are students from all over the world.
8 Coffee with milk is **popular** in my country. Everyone drinks it. It's really good.

a _____ (n) a person who travels and visits places for fun

b _____ (adj) made with new ideas and designs

c _____ (n) land with water all around it

d _____ (n) an area of sand or rocks next to a sea, ocean, or lake

e _____ (n) the most important city in a country, where the government is

f _____ (adj) known by many people

g _____ (adj) liked by many people

h _____ (adj) relating to or involving two or more countries

Zócalo Square in Mexico City

2 USING YOUR KNOWLEDGE **Ask and answer the questions with a partner. Then write your answers in the chart below.**

1 What is the name of your country?
2 What is the capital of your country?
3 How many people do you think live in your country?
4 What is the climate in your country?
5 What languages do people speak in your country?
6 What types of businesses are the most important in your country?

Fact File	
Name of country	
Capital	
Population	
Climate	
Languages	
Businesses	

THE MALDIVES – AN OVERVIEW

WHY GO TO THE MALDIVES?

1 The Maldives are **islands** in the Indian Ocean. The islands are near Sri Lanka. The Maldives are **famous** for their good climate, beautiful **beaches**, and warm seas.

2 There are 370,000 people in the Maldives. Most people live on small islands.

3 The **capital** of the Maldives is Malé. It is a **modern** city with an **international** airport and a big harbor[1].

4 People in Malé speak English and Dhivehi. English is useful because many **tourists** come here.

5 Tourism and fishing are the most important businesses in the Maldives. There are many hotels. Many people work there. Others work as fishermen or in fish factories[2]. The currency[3] is the rufiyaa.

> ❝
> The Maldives are famous for their good climate, beautiful beaches, and warm seas.

Fishing is popular in the Maldives.

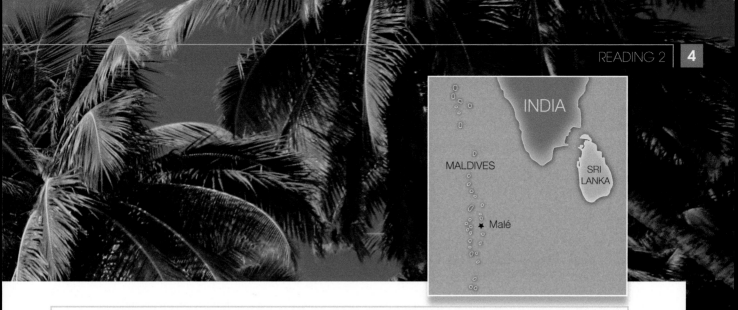

MEET THE LOCALS *Ahmed Faiz, 19*

6 I live on an island south of Malé. Life on my island is very simple. There are some stores, and there is one mosque. We speak Dhivehi, but we also learn English in high school. It is a nice place to live.

7 The Maldives are famous for their fish. There is a **popular** fish soup here. It is called *garudiya*. It is delicious.

8 People in the Maldives like to swim and dive.

Ahmed Faiz

FACT FILE

FULL NAME: Republic of Maldives

POPULATION: 370,000

CAPITAL: Malé

GEOGRAPHY: 1,190 islands

CLIMATE: good, warm, average
     temperature 86° F (30° C)

LANGUAGES: Dhivehi and English

RELIGION: Islam

CURRENCY: rufiyaa

INDUSTRY[4]: tourism and fishing

[1]**harbor** (n) area of water next to land where ships and boats can be safely kept

[2]**factories** (n) buildings where a large amount of things or products are made

[3]**currency** (n) the money a country or countries use

[4]**industry** (n) types of businesses

READING FOR MAIN IDEAS

Each paragraph in a text has a *topic* and a *main idea*. The topic is what the paragraph is about. The main idea tells the most important idea about the topic.

> Tourism and fishing are the most important businesses in the Maldives. There are many hotels. Many people work there. Others work as fishermen or in fish factories. The currency is the rufiyaa.

The topic here is *tourism and fishing*. The main idea is that *tourism and fishing are the most important businesses in the Maldives.*

3 TAKING NOTES **Read the text about the Maldives on pages 78–79. Write the topics and the main ideas next to the paragraph numbers from the text.**

paragraph	topic	main idea
1		
2		
3		
4		
5		
6		
7		
8		

🔆 CRITICAL THINKING

4 SYNTHESIZING **Work with a partner. Use ideas from Reading 1 and Reading 2 to answer the questions.**

UNDERSTAND

Why do tourists go to the Maldives?

ANALYZE

Do you want to visit the Maldives? Why or why not?

EVALUATE

Why are people interested in different countries?

🔗 COLLABORATION

5 **A** Work with a partner. Interview a local person, a teacher, or a classmate. Ask the questions and take notes on the answers.

- What is your name?
- What do you do?
- Where do you live?
- What kind of food is popular there?
- What do people do there in their free time?

B Write a "Meet the Locals" text from your interview notes. Use Reading 2 as a model. Include photos.

C Present your text and photos to the class.

SUPERLATIVE ADJECTIVES

LANGUAGE

Superlative adjectives describe how a person or thing in a group is different from all the others. Superlative adjectives have different forms.

Use *the* before a superlative adjective.

For one-syllable adjectives, add *-est*.

long → longest

The **longest** river is in Africa.

For one-syllable adjectives ending in *-e*, add *-st*.

blue → bluest

The **bluest** water is the Caribbean Sea.

For adjectives that end in one vowel + one consonant, double the consonant and add *-est*.

big → biggest   hot → hottest

The capital has **the biggest** population.

For adjectives with two or more syllables that end in *-y*, change *y* to *i* and add *-est*.

friendly → friendliest

The Maldives have **the friendliest** people.

For adjectives with two or more syllables, add *the most* before the adjective.

important → the most important   popular → the most popular

Tourism and fishing are **the most important** businesses in the Maldives.

Some adjectives have irregular superlative forms.

good → the best   bad → the worst

1 **Rewrite the sentences using the superlative form of the adjectives in bold.**

1   The Maldives have a **warm** climate.
    The Maldives have the warmest climate.

2   The Missouri River in the United States is **long**.

_____

3   The beaches in the Maldives are **beautiful**.

_____

4   A **popular** dish in the Maldives is fish soup.

_____

NOUN PHRASES WITH *OF*

LANGUAGE

One type of noun phrase is a noun + *of* + a noun.

Bogota is **the capital of Colombia**. Paris is in **the center of the country**.
This book is about **the history of Japan**.

2 **Match the sentence halves.**

1	The book is a history	a	of the United States.
2	The capital	b	of Asia.
3	The dollar is the currency	c	of Canada are English and French.
4	The main languages	d	of maps.
5	Al-Idrisi's map shows parts	e	of the Maldives is Malé.

VOCABULARY FOR PLACES

3 **Write the words from the box in the correct places on the picture.**

beach   cliff   desert   farm   field   forest   hill   mountains   sea   valley

WATCH AND LISTEN

1   2   3   4

PREPARING TO WATCH

1 ACTIVATING YOUR KNOWLEDGE **Work with a partner and answer the questions.**

1   What makes a place special?
2   Why do people like to visit special places?
3   What special place would you like to visit? Why?

2 PREDICTING CONTENT USING VISUALS **Look at the pictures from the video. Put the words in order to make sentences.**

1   monkey / There is / in the forest /.
2   in the trees / a space / There is /.
3   are growing / Plants / in the water /.
4   in the water / is swimming / A man /.

WHILE WATCHING

▶ **3** UNDERSTANDING MAIN IDEAS **Watch the video. Check (✓) the true statements.**

1   ☐   There aren't many rich, green forests in the Yucatán.
2   ☐   The people in Mexico call the holes in the forests *cenotes*.
3   ☐   These holes are made of wood.
4   ☐   The scientist studies the trees there.
5   ☐   In the Yucatán, *cenotes* are the only places to find fresh water.
6   ☐   Most of the plants and animals live at the top of the *cenotes*.

▶ **4** UNDERSTANDING DETAILS **Watch again. Fill in the blanks with the missing words.**

1 These amazing holes are the only spaces in the _____.

2 For Olmo, the *cenotes* are very _____.

3 _____ is very important in the Yucatán.

4 *Cenotes* help the _____ and plants in the forest live.

5 When Olmo swims far into the cave, it gets _____ and dark.

5 MAKING INFERENCES **Circle the correct word or phrase.**

1 *Cenotes* are *very / not* important in the Yucatán.
2 Animals and plants *need / die in* the *cenotes*.
3 There *is / is no* life in the water.
4 It is *safe / dangerous* to swim far into the cave.

☼ CRITICAL THINKING

6 Work with a partner and answer the questions.

APPLY	ANALYZE	EVALUATE
What special places are there in your country? Describe them.	Would you like to visit the *cenotes*? Why or why not?	Would you like to swim in a cave? Why or why not?

COLLABORATION

7 A Work with a partner. Which place is more fun to visit:

• a place, such as a city or beach resort, that is popular with tourists?

• a quiet place in the country that is not popular with tourists?

Think of at least three reasons to support your answers.

B Share your ideas with the class. Write the five best reasons you hear.

C As a class, vote on the best type of place to visit.

JOBS

LEARNING OBJECTIVES

Key Reading Skill	Reading for details
Additional Reading Skills	Understanding key vocabulary; using your knowledge; previewing; scanning to find information; taking notes; reading for main ideas; synthesizing
Language Development	Vocabulary for jobs; adjective phrases

ACTIVATE YOUR KNOWLEDGE

Ask and answer the questions with a partner.

1 What do you think the people's jobs are?

2 Do you want this job? Why or why not?

3 What makes a job good?

4 What job do you want? What job do you not want?

PREPARING TO READ

1 UNDERSTANDING KEY VOCABULARY **Read the sentences. Choose the best definition for the words in bold.**

1 I am **in shape**. I run every day and ride my bike to work.
   a in good health; strong
   b have a lot of money

2 My mom is a doctor. She works at a **hospital**.
   a a place where people who are sick or hurt go for help
   b a place where people go to study and learn

3 Miriam needs two teaspoons of **medicine**. She is not feeling well.
   a a sandwich or a salad
   b something you take to feel better

4 Oscar is a **pilot**. He learned to fly planes and did well on a flying test.
   a a person who teaches children
   b a person who flies an airplane

5 Basketball players get good **pay**. They make millions of dollars a year.
   a the money you receive for doing a job
   b the feeling you get from doing good work

6 I have **friendly** teachers. They always say "hi" and smile when I see them.
   a nice and kind
   b not nice or kind

7 The **nurse** checked the boy's temperature. He was not feeling well.
   a a person who helps doctors and takes care of people
   b a person who helps children learn at school

8 I am **healthy**. I eat food that is good for me. I get sleep. I take care of myself.
   a quick to understand; smart
   b being well; not sick

2 USING YOUR KNOWLEDGE **Ask and answer the questions with a partner.**

1 Where do you find information about jobs?
2 What information do you want to know before you take a job?
3 What makes someone good at his or her job?

3 PREVIEWING **Look at the texts on pages 90–91. Where are they from?**

a a website for tourists
b a website for jobs
c a website for students

4 Look at the photos on pages 90–91. What do they show?

a great places in Vancouver
b different types of schools
c locations of different jobs

FIND_MY_JOB.COM

FIND A JOB   GET HELP!   UPLOAD YOUR RÉSUMÉ

A YOUR SEARCH

Area(s): Medicine

Job(s): Nurse

✉ Email me jobs like this

📶 RSS Feeds

Location[1]: Vancouver, British Columbia, Canada

Vancouver Hospital

Vancouver Hospital is part of the British Columbia University School of **Medicine**. We teach doctors and **nurses**.

We are looking for a nurse to work at the **hospital** and teach student nurses. You have to work early mornings and late nights.

You must have ten years of experience[2]. You must also speak Chinese and English.

Pay: $4,800 per month

Schedule: Monday–Friday and some weekends

Come to Vancouver!

Fly with the best in the west!

B YOUR SEARCH

Area(s): Aviation
Job(s): Pilot
✉ Email me jobs like this
🔊 RSS Feeds
Location: Denver,
Colorado,
United States

FlyHigh Air Transport Company

FlyHigh is a small company in Denver, Colorado. We have private[3] flights throughout the United States.

We are looking for a **pilot**. All our pilots are **friendly** and speak English and Spanish.

You must have two years of experience. You have to work weekends. You must be **healthy** and **in shape**.

Pay: $130–180 per hour

Schedule: 10–15 hours per week

C YOUR SEARCH

Area(s): Education
Job(s): Teacher
✉ Email me jobs like this
🔊 RSS Feeds
Location: Shelburne,
Nova Scotia, Canada

Shelburne Elementary School

Shelburne is a private school in Nova Scotia. Our teachers are friendly and interested in helping children.

We are looking for a math teacher to teach grades 1–3. You must have a university education. You must speak English.

Pay: $48,000 per year

Schedule: September–June

Shelburne Elementary is a private school in beautiful Nova Scotia.

[1]**location** (n) a place
[2]**experience** (n) what you know from doing your job
[3]**private** (adj) belongs to one person or group

5 SCANNING TO FIND INFORMATION **Read the questions below. Scan Reading 1. Underline the answers in the text, and write them in the blanks below.**

1 What is the pay for the pilot? _____

2 What country is the nurse's job in? _____

3 What is the teacher's schedule? _____

4 Which job is in Denver? _____

6 TAKING NOTES **Read the job postings on pages 90–91. Complete the chart.**

	text A	text B	text C
job			
place of work			
pay			
schedule			

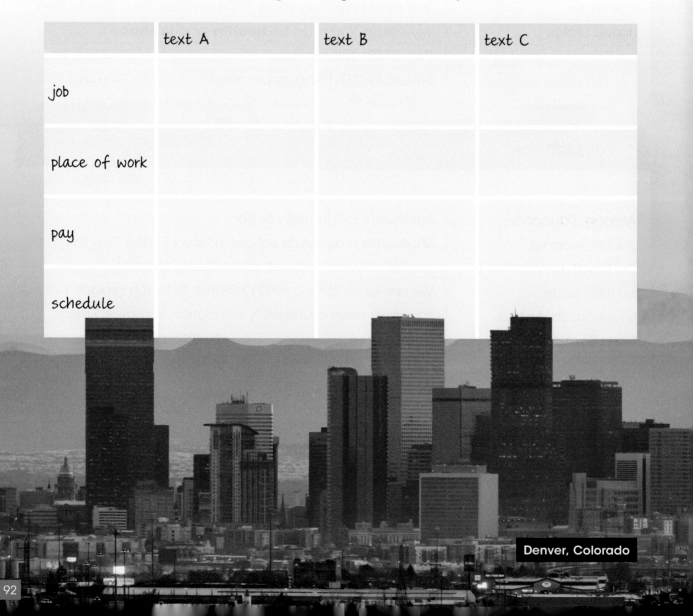

Denver, Colorado

⚒ SKILLS

READING FOR DETAILS

Reading for details means looking for key words and information that tell you about the main idea. One way of reading for details is to follow the steps below:

- Ask a question. (e.g., *What is the job at Vancouver Hospital?*)
- Scan the text to find key words. (e.g., *Vancouver, teach, nurses*)
- Read the sentences in the paragraph with the key words. (e.g., *We are looking for a nurse to work at the hospital and teach student nurses.*)

7 READING FOR DETAILS **Read the statements. Write *T* (true) or *F* (false). Correct the false statements.**

_____ 1 The pilot at FlyHigh must speak two languages.

_____ 2 The teacher at Shelburne Elementary School has to teach grade 12.

_____ 3 The nurse at Vancouver Hospital must have ten years of experience.

_____ 4 Pilots at FlyHigh are paid per hour.

_____ 5 The nurse at Vancouver Hospital must speak two languages.

💡 CRITICAL THINKING

8 Work with a partner. Ask and answer the questions.

UNDERSTAND

Which jobs need someone who is friendly?

ANALYZE

Why do some jobs ask you to speak more than one language?

EVALUATE

Which job from Reading 1 do you want? Why?

🤝 COLLABORATION

9 A Work with a partner. Think of a job in your town or city. Write the name of the job, the place of work, the pay, and the schedule in your notebook. If necessary, do some research online.

B Change partners and compare your jobs. Answer the questions.

- Which job is better?
- Which job do you want? Why?

C Repeat step B with other classmates.

PREPARING TO READ

1 UNDERSTANDING KEY VOCABULARY **Read the sentences. Write the words and phrases in bold next to the definitions.**

1 Science is very **interesting**. There is so much to learn and know.

2 I work for a **company** that makes computers.

3 I'm a math **teacher**. I teach calculus to students at Halifax School.

4 My university has a music **center**. People take music classes and see music shows there.

5 My sister is very **good at** basketball. She is the best player on the team.

6 I need to do well in **high school** so I can go to a good university.

7 My mom is an **engineer**. She designs and builds parts for cars.

8 School is **great**. I really like it, and I'm learning a lot. It's going well.

a _____ (n) a person who designs and builds things

b _____ (n) an organization that sells something to make money

c _____ (n) a school for children about 15 to 18 years old

What jobs are you interested in?

d _____ (adj) able to do something well

e _____ (n) a place with a special purpose

f _____ (adj) very good; excellent

g _____ (n) a person who helps others to learn

h _____ (adj) getting your attention because it is exciting; not boring

2 USING YOUR KNOWLEDGE **Think about the emails you write to your friends.**

1 Why do you write them?
2 What do you write about?
3 Is your language the same when you write as when you speak?

3 Work with a partner. Compare your answers in Exercise 2. What is the same? What is different?

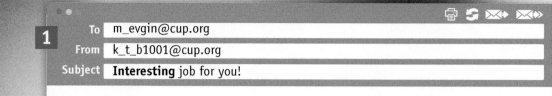

To	m_evgin@cup.org
From	k_t_b1001@cup.org
Subject	**Interesting** job for you!

Hi, Meng!

I found a **great** job for you. It's for a dance **teacher**. The job is at David Allen's Dance **Center** in Allentown.

You have to get up early in the morning. There are 12 students in each group. You have to be very friendly and **good at** dancing. The pay is very good – they pay $28 an hour. You don't have to work on Saturday or Sunday.

I think you'll like this job. Here's the link[1]:

www.dancecompany.org/dance-teacher

Talk to you soon!
Karel

Take classes in our new center!

[1]link (n) a word or phrase on a website that takes you to another website
[2]software (n) the instructions that control what a computer can do; computer program

To erik1221@cup.org
From ingrid_soljberg@cup.org
Subject IT'S MOM – LOOK AT THIS JOB!

2

Erik,

I found a great job for you. It's in Oslo, and I know you want to live there. Here's the link

www.itcompany.org/jobs.

I know this **company**.
The job is for a software[2] **engineer**. They pay $65,150 a year!
You must have studied computer science in college, and you have to have 2 years of experience. It also says that you must know some Norwegian. You don't have to speak Norwegian a lot, so it's OK for you.

Let me know what you think!

Love,
Mom

Oslo
is a great place to live!

To akhrorova_daria@cup.org
From olly_murgatroyd@cup.org
Subject Do you want a job in a great country?

3

Dear Daria,

I hope you're well. I have a great job for you. I think you'll like it. It's in South Korea! I know you love Korean food.

The job is in Yeonggwang. It's a small town in the south of the country.

The job is at a **high school**. You have to teach English and French to grades 10 to 12. You speak English and French (and Russian!).

You don't have to speak Korean, so this is a great job for you. You have to work many hours every day. But you are a very serious teacher. I know you work hard.

Here's the link:

www.skoreajobs.com/Education/HS/Languages

Good luck!
Oliver

**Enjoy Korean food
at
Gamami Beach!**

4 SCANNING TO FIND INFORMATION **Scan the texts on pages 96–97. Write the correct information in the blanks.**

1   The email to Meng is about a job as a _____ .

2   There are _____ students in a dance class at the center.

3   The email to Erik is about a job as a _____ .

4   The pay for Erik's job is $ _____ a year.

5   The job for Daria is in _____ .

6   Daria must teach grades _____ to _____ .

5 READING FOR MAIN IDEAS **Choose the answer that best states the main ideas.**

a   Each email is from a company. The company gives information about a job.

b   Each email is about a teaching job. The emails talk about the languages the person needs to speak.

c   Each email is from a family member or friend. The person talks about a job.

d   Each email is from a person looking for a job. The person says why the job is good.

6 READING FOR DETAILS **Read the texts again. Write *M* (Meng), *E* (Erik), or *D* (Daria) next to the statements.**

1   He or she must be good at dancing. _____

2   He or she has to teach two languages. _____

3   He or she must have two years of experience. _____

4   He or she has to get up early. _____

5   He or she must work many hours every day. _____

CRITICAL THINKING

7 SYNTHESIZING **Work with a partner. Use ideas from Reading 1 and Reading 2 to answer the questions.**

UNDERSTAND	APPLY	ANALYZE	EVALUATE
Which of the jobs would you be good at? Why?	Which of the jobs do you need to be healthy and in shape for? Why?	What else does each job need a person to be good at?	What information is important to know about a job?

COLLABORATION

8 **A** Work in a small group. Look at the jobs in Reading 2. As a group, make a list of the tasks each person does every day.

B Who in your group has the skills for each job? Match each group member with a job from Reading 2.

C Share your lists with the class. Tell the class why each person is good for the job.

LANGUAGE DEVELOPMENT

VOCABULARY FOR JOBS

1 **Make sentences about jobs. Write the verb phrases from the box in the correct places in column B of the chart.**

> grows food   writes news stories
> plays on a sports team   teaches children
> ~~gives people medicine~~
> teaches dance   takes care of sick people
> creates software for computers   teaches languages
> manages people

A jobs	B activities	C locations
1 A farmer		on a farm.
2 A manager		
3 A doctor	gives people medicine	
4 A journalist		in towns, cities, and different countries.
5 A software engineer		
6 A basketball player		in big cities.
7 A school teacher		
8 A dance teacher		
9 A nurse		
10 A language teacher		

2 Write the prepositional phrases from the box in the correct places in column C of the chart. The phrases may be used more than once.

> in a hospital.   in an office.   in a school.
> in a center.   in a company.

ADJECTIVE PHRASES

LANGUAGE

An *adjective phrase* describes the subject of the sentence. The adjective phrase comes after a form of the verb *be*. One type of adjective phrase is *very* + adjective.

Software engineers have to be **very smart**. Nurses must be **very kind**.

Another type of adjective phrase is adjective + *and* + adjective.

Pilots must be **healthy and in shape**. Nurses have to be **kind and helpful**.

Another type of adjective phrase is *good at* + noun or *good with* + noun.

The teacher has to be **good at math**. Nurses must be **good with people**.

Usually people are *good at* a subject and *good with* a person or object.

3 Read the sentences and circle the best words and phrases.

1 Dance teachers have to be *interesting / healthy and strong*. They are moving around all day!

2 Doctors must be *very smart / very healthy and strong*. There is a lot to know about medicine.

3 Nurses have to be *friendly / strong*. They work with people.

4 Farmers have to be *strong / friendly*. They work with animals and equipment.

4 Circle the correct preposition in each sentence.

1 An elementary school teacher has to be good *at / with* children.

2 A software engineer needs to be good *at / with* computers.

3 A nurse needs to be good *at / with* people.

4 A French and Spanish teacher needs to be good *at / with* languages.

5 A journalist needs to be good *at / with* writing.

WATCH AND LISTEN

GLOSSARY

copper (n) a soft, red-brown metal used to make wires, pipes, etc.
mine (n) a hole in the ground where people dig out gold, coal, etc.
produce (v) to make or grow something
wire (n) a long, very thin piece of metal
dig (v) to make a hole in the ground by moving the dirt away
giant (adj) very big

PREPARING TO WATCH

1 ACTIVATING YOUR KNOWLEDGE **Work with a partner and answer the questions.**

1 Do you work? What do you do?
2 What are some unusual jobs?
3 What are some dangerous jobs?
4 Would you like to have an unusual job? Why or why not?

2 PREDICTING CONTENT USING VISUALS **Look at the pictures from the video. Match the sentence halves.**

1 There is a large	a much bigger than the man.
2 The truck is carrying	b are flying in the air.
3 The truck is	c hole in the ground.
4 The dirt and rocks	d a lot of rocks and dirt.

WHILE WATCHING

3 UNDERSTANDING MAIN IDEAS **Watch the video. Write _T_ (true) or _F_ (false) next to the statements. Correct the false statements.**

_____ 1 The Bingham mine is in Utah.

_____ 2 The mine produces enough copper wires for all the homes in Canada.

_____ 3 We use copper wires in a lot of different places.

_____ 4 The trucks work 12 hours a day.

▶ **4** UNDERSTANDING DETAILS **Watch again. Circle the words you hear.**

1   It is the *largest / longest* mine of its kind in the world.

2   It is almost *one mile / two-and-a-half miles* deep.

3   The rocks contain a *large / small* amount of copper.

4   They also use something *stronger / weaker* to get the rocks and copper out of the ground.

5 MAKING INFERENCES **Check (✓) the sentences about work in the Bingham mine. Give reasons for your answers.**

1   ☐   It is difficult.

2   ☐   It can be dangerous.

3   ☐   The truck drivers work in the office for half of the day.

4   ☐   The operations manager has an important job.

5   ☐   Finding copper can take a long time.

6   ☐   There are many mines in Utah.

☼ CRITICAL THINKING

6   **Work with a partner and answer the questions.**

APPLY	APPLY	ANALYZE
Is working in the Bingham mine an interesting job? Why or why not?	Are there any mines in your country or region? What do they produce?	What other jobs are similar to working in a mine?

🗫 COLLABORATION

7   **A**   Work with a partner. Make a posting for a job in the video. Use Reading 1 as a model. Choose one:

• operations manager   • truck driver   • miner

B   Share your job posting with the class on an online discussion board or in your classroom.

C   Answer one of the job postings in an email. Think about:

• Why do you want the job?

• Why are you good at the job?

• What other information do you want to know about the job?

HOMES AND BUILDINGS

LEARNING OBJECTIVES

Key Reading Skill	Predicting content using visuals
Additional Reading Skills	Understanding key vocabulary; using your knowledge; scanning to find information; reading for main ideas; reading for details; annotating; synthesizing
Language Development	Pronouns; vocabulary for buildings; adjectives for buildings

ACTIVATE YOUR KNOWLEDGE

Work with a partner. Ask and answer the questions below.

1 Do you think this town looks like a nice place to live? Why or why not?

2 How is this town like your town or city? How is it different?

3 Do you like being in very big cities? Why or why not?

PREPARING TO READ

1 UNDERSTANDING KEY VOCABULARY **Read the sentences. Write the words in bold below the photos.**

1 In a **garden**, you grow flowers and plants.
2 Children drink out of **plastic** cups.
3 Cities have **tall** buildings.
4 Tables and chairs are made of **wood**.
5 The **roof** on our house is red.
6 I have a picture on the **wall**.
7 The sun shines through the **window**.
8 Be careful. **Glass** can break.

2 USING YOUR KNOWLEDGE **Ask and answer the questions with a partner.**

1 What do you like about your home?

2 What kind of home do you want to live in?

3 What makes a home a good place to live?

✎ SKILLS

PREDICTING CONTENT USING VISUALS

Visuals can be photographs, pictures, graphs, or charts. You can use the visuals to help you understand the topic of the text.

---

3 PREDICTING CONTENT USING VISUALS **Look at the photos, title, and headings on pages 108–109. Choose the correct answer.**

1 What is this text?

   a an interview

   b a book review

   c a story

2 Where is the text from?

   a a textbook

   b a web site

   c a magazine

3 What will the architect talk about?

   a buildings in the United States

   b very old buildings

   c buildings around the world

4 What kinds of buildings does the architect design?

   a office buildings

   b homes

   c schools

ARCHITECT'S WORLD
EXPERT INTERVIEW

The architect, Michael Chan, makes drawings for houses.

1   ***Professor Michael Chan*** *teaches design to architects at the London School of Architecture. He has been at the school for 30 years. There have been many changes in home design in the last 30 years. This week, Michael Chan tells us more about new home design around the world.*

Japanese roof house

2 **Architect's World:** What are your favorite home designs?
Michael Chan: I really like Japanese designs. Many people in Japan build interesting houses. For example, the roof house is very **tall** and has a steep[1] **roof**. The **windows** on the roof are different sizes. Inside the house, the rooms are very narrow[2], and the ceilings[3] are very high. It is simple and very small inside.

garden home with plants

3 **AW:** What do you think about "green"[4] homes?
MC: It is very important to build houses that are good for the Earth. My favorite example is a house in Saigon, Vietnam. It is a "garden home." This house is in the middle of a busy city, but there are plants everywhere. From the street, people see a tall **garden**. But, in fact, it is a house. There are plants and trees in front of the glass **walls**. There is also a small garden on top of the roof. You can put chairs and a table there and enjoy tea with your family.

mirror house

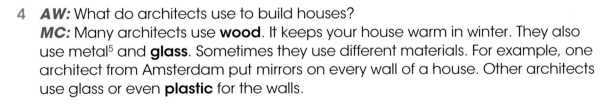
" It is very important to build houses that are good for the Earth.

4 **AW:** What do architects use to build houses?
MC: Many architects use **wood**. It keeps your house warm in winter. They also use metal[5] and **glass**. Sometimes they use different materials. For example, one architect from Amsterdam put mirrors on every wall of a house. Other architects use glass or even **plastic** for the walls.

[1]steep (adj) goes down very quickly and almost straight down

[2]narrow (adj) not much space from one side to the other

[3]ceilings (n) the inside top of a room that you see when you look up

[4]green (adj) something that is good for the Earth and does not use a lot of energy

[5]metal (adj) a hard and shiny material, such as iron or gold

4 SCANNING TO FIND INFORMATION **Read the text on pages 108–109. Check (✓) the boxes in the chart that are true for the two houses.**

	windows are different sizes	has glass walls	has a small garden on the roof	rooms are narrow
Japanese roof house				
Vietnamese "garden home"				

5 READING FOR MAIN IDEAS **Match the sentence parts to create a main idea.**

1 Michael Chan likes

2 Green architecture is

3 Architects make homes out of

a metal, wood, glass, and plastic.

b good for the Earth.

c unusual and interesting homes.

6 READING FOR DETAILS **Read the text again. Write _T_ (true) or _F_ (false) next to the statements. Correct the false statements.**

_____ 1 Professor Chan's favorite home designs are Korean.

_____ 2 The roof house has small and narrow rooms.

_____ 3 Professor Chan says it is important to build more homes in Vietnam.

_____ 4 The "garden home" is in the center of a big city.

_____ 5 Gardens and plants are good for the Earth.

_____ 6 In Amsterdam, many architects put mirrors on the walls.

💡 CRITICAL THINKING

7 **Ask and answer the questions with a partner.**

UNDERSTAND	APPLY	ANALYZE
What design ideas are important to Michael Chan?	Why do you think the architect from Amsterdam used mirrors?	What do you think makes a home good for the Earth?

🧠 COLLABORATION

8 **A** Work with a partner. List the questions from the interview on pages 108–109. Add 2 more questions to ask your partner about the home designs and ideas in the text.

- _____

- _____

- _____

- _____

- _____

   B Take turns interviewing each other about the different designs and ideas in the text. Use your own words to answer the questions.

   C Change partners. Repeat step B.

More architects are designing garden homes.

PREPARING TO READ

1 UNDERSTANDING KEY VOCABULARY **Read the sentences. Write the words in bold next to the correct definitions.**

1 The car is too **expensive**. I don't have the money to buy it.
2 The **buildings** in my city are made of metal and glass – both the stores and the offices.
3 You can take an **elevator** to the top of the building. It is very high!
4 I live in an **apartment** on the fourth floor.
5 How much does this TV **cost**? I can't see the price.
6 A plane ticket to Boston is very **cheap**! I bought it for only $54!

a _____ (adj) costing a lot of money

b _____ (n) a house, school, office, or store with a roof and walls

c _____ (adj) costing little money

d _____ (n) a set of rooms for someone to live in on one level of a building or house

e _____ (v) to have an amount of money as a price that someone must pay

f _____ (n) a machine, like a small room, that carries people straight up or down in a tall building

What is too expensive for you to buy?

2 USING YOUR KNOWLEDGE **Tell a partner if you agree or disagree with each statement. Explain why.**

1 It's important for the buildings in a city to look interesting.
2 Tall buildings are better than small buildings.
3 It is fun to be high up in a building.
4 The best building designs are expensive.
5 Most buildings are good for the earth.
6 Cities with tall buildings are important.
7 People visit a city to see its buildings.
8 It cost a lot of money to build a tall building.
9 It is best to live in a tall building.
10 Every city should have tall buildings.

3 PREDICTING CONTENT USING VISUALS **Look at the title, photos, and headings on pages 114–115. Choose the correct answers.**

1 What is the purpose of this text?
   a to tell a story
   b to share the writer's feelings
   c to give facts and information

2 What question will the text answer?
   a How do you build a skyscraper?
   b What is a skyscraper?
   c Who designs skyscrapers?

3 What skyscrapers will the text discuss?
   a skyscrapers in Shanghai
   b very tall skyscrapers
   c skyscrapers in the future

SKYSCRAPERS:
BUILDINGS THAT TOUCH THE SKY

What Are Skyscrapers?

1 Skyscrapers are very tall **buildings**. They are usually more than 984 feet (300 meters) tall. You can see skyscrapers in cities around the world. Many countries build skyscrapers so tourists go there. There are many skyscrapers in Asia, the Middle East, the Americas, and Europe. Inside a skyscraper, there are offices, stores, restaurants, and **apartments**.

What Are Some Famous Skyscrapers?

2 The Empire State Building in New York is a world-famous skyscraper. It has two million visitors every year. It is popular with tourists, but there are taller and more modern skyscrapers in the Middle East and in Asia. The Shanghai World Financial Center, One World Trade Center in New York City, and the Burj Khalifa in Dubai are taller than the Empire State Building. The Burj Khalifa is taller than the Shanghai World Financial Center and One World Trade Center. One World Trade Center is taller than the Shanghai World Financial Center. One World Trade Center is more modern than the other two buildings. It opened in 2014.

Shanghai World Financial Center, 2008 (1,614 feet)

How Expensive Are Skyscrapers?

3 Skyscrapers are very **expensive**. They **cost** more money than other buildings. The Burj Khalifa cost $1,500,000,000 to build. It was more expensive than the Shanghai World Financial Center ($850,000,000), but it was **cheaper** than One World Trade Center. One World Trade Center cost $3,900,000,000.

What Is Inside a Skyscraper?

4 The Burj Khalifa has 163 floors. This is more than One World Trade Center or the Shanghai World Financial Center. One World Trade Center has 104 floors and the Shanghai World Financial Center has 101 floors. All skyscrapers have **elevators**. The Burj Khalifa has more elevators than One World Trade Center or the Shanghai World Financial Center. It has 57 elevators. One World Trade Center has 54 elevators, but the Shanghai World Financial Center has fewer. It only has 31. Many skyscrapers also have shopping malls inside them. A lot of people come to shop every day.

One World Trade Center, 2014 (1,776 feet)

Burj Khalifa, 2010 (2,717 feet)

4 SCANNING TO FIND INFORMATION **Scan the report on pages 114–115, and complete the chart.**

	Shanghai World Financial Center	One World Trade Center	Burj Khalifa
A city	Shanghai	New York	(1) _____
B height (ft)	(2) _____	(3) _____	2,717
C year	2008	2014	2010
D number of floors	(4) _____	104	163
E number of elevators	(5) _____	54	57
F cost (USD)	$850,000,000	(6) $ _____	$1,500,000,000

5 ANNOTATING **Read the report. Follow the directions to annotate it.**

1 Underline the four main questions the text asks.

2 Underline key words in each paragraph that answer the question.

3 Compare your answers with a partner.

🔅 CRITICAL THINKING

6 SYNTHESIZING **Work with a partner. Use ideas from Reading 1 and Reading 2 to answer the questions.**

APPLY	ANALYZE	EVALUATE
Which building do you think was the most expensive to build? Why do you think it was so expensive?	Why do you think skyscrapers need so many elevators?	What information do architects need to make a building or a home?

🔗 COLLABORATION

7 **A** Work in a small group. Find information about a different skyscraper, and complete the chart. If necessary, go online and do some research.

Name of building:	
city	
height	
year	
number of floors	
number of elevators	
cost	

B Write a paragraph about your building. Use Reading 2 as a model. Include the following information:

- How tall is your building? Compare its height to a building in the article.

- How much did your building cost? Compare its cost to a building in the article.

- How many elevators does the building have? Compare that number to a building in the article.

C Compare your paragraph with another group.

LANGUAGE DEVELOPMENT

PRONOUNS

LANGUAGE

You can match *pronouns* to nouns to help you understand a text.

Skyscrapers are very tall buildings. **They** [They = Skyscrapers] are usually more than 984 ft (300 m) tall.

The Empire State Building in New York is a world-famous skyscraper.

It [It = The Empire State Building] has two million visitors every year.

1 Review the text on pages 114–115 again. Match the words and phrases in the box to the pronouns in bold in the sentences.

> Burj Khalifa   One World Trade Center
> Shanghai World Financial Center   skyscrapers

1 **It** was more expensive than the Shanghai World Financial Center ($850,000,000). _____

2 **It** opened in 2014. _____

3 **They** cost more money than other buildings. _____

4 **It** has only 31 elevators. _____

VOCABULARY FOR BUILDINGS

2 Read the sentences and write the words from the box in the blanks.

> ceiling   elevators   entrance   exit
> parking lot   shopping mall   stairs

The John Hancock Center in Chicago is one of the tallest buildings in North America.

1 There are over 520 different stores in the Mall of America, which

is a _____ in Minnesota.

2 The John Hancock Center in Chicago has a race up the building.

People run up the _____ .

3 Skyscrapers often have one main _____ at the front of the building. It is also the _____ . You leave from there, too.

4 Each floor in the One World Trade Center is nine feet high from floor to _____ .

5 There are 1,100 parking spaces in the _____ at Shanghai World Financial Center.

6 Skyscrapers must have _____ . They are too tall for people to walk up the stairs.

ADJECTIVES FOR BUILDINGS

3 Match the adjectives to their opposites.

1 traditional   a ugly

2 old   b cheap

3 expensive   c modern

4 beautiful   d new

4 Write the adjectives from the box in the correct blanks.

| beautiful   cheap   expensive   modern   traditional   ugly |

1 It is _____ to build skyscrapers. They are not cheap.

2 Buildings with glass look _____ . They shine in the sun.

3 Skyscrapers are _____ buildings. They are new and interesting.

4 Some homes in China are _____ . They look like homes from the past.

5 It is hard to find a _____ apartment in the city. They cost too much money.

6 Most people like skyscrapers, but I think they are _____ . I prefer small buildings and more traditional designs.

WATCH AND LISTEN

PREPARING TO WATCH

1 ACTIVATING YOUR KNOWLEDGE **Work with a partner. Write the name of a famous tall building for each country.**

Canada	Mexico	Italy	Dubai, UAE	China

2 PREDICTING CONTENT USING VISUALS **Look at the pictures from the video. Match the pictures (1–4) to the countries.**

a England _____

b United States _____

c France _____

d Egypt _____

WHILE WATCHING

▶ 3 UNDERSTANDING MAIN IDEAS **Watch the video. Put the buildings in order (1–5) from the oldest to the newest.**

a Lincoln Cathedral _____

b Eiffel Tower _____

c Great Pyramid _____

d Taipei 101 _____

e Chrysler Building _____

4 UNDERSTANDING DETAILS **Watch again. Circle the correct answer.**

1 The Great Pyramid of Egypt is *445 / 455* feet tall.
2 The Lincoln Cathedral was 46 feet taller than the *Great Pyramid / Eiffel Tower*.
3 The Chrysler Building used *stone / steel* to make it the tallest skyscraper in 1930.
4 The Petronas Towers in Kuala Lumpur, Malaysia are made of glass, steel, and *stone / concrete*.

5 MAKING INFERENCES **Using the information in the video, check (✓) the true statements.**

1 ☐ Buildings are getting taller.
2 ☐ Buildings do not change very much.
3 ☐ New materials help us build taller buildings.
4 ☐ New buildings use more glass than old buildings.
5 ☐ Skyscrapers are common in large cities.
6 ☐ There will be more skyscrapers in the future.

☼ CRITICAL THINKING

6 SYNTHESIZING **Work with a partner and answer the questions.**

APPLY

Describe the tallest building in your city.

APPLY

Have you visited any of the buildings in the video? If so, which one(s)?

ANALYZE

Which building in this unit would you like to visit the most? Why?

☙ COLLABORATION

7 A Work in a small group. Choose three buildings from this unit: one from Reading 1, one from Reading 2, and one from the video. Take notes about each building in a chart. Include a description and your opinion of each building.

1	2	3

B Use your notes to prepare a two-minute group podcast. Use the video as a model. Then record or present your podcast to the class.

FOOD AND CULTURE

LEARNING OBJECTIVES

Key Reading Skill	Taking notes
Additional Reading Skills	Understanding key vocabulary; using your knowledge; previewing; reading for main ideas; scanning to find information; reading for details; synthesizing
Language Development	Vocabulary about food; count and noncount nouns

ACTIVATE YOUR KNOWLEDGE

Work with a partner. Ask and answer the questions.

1. Where are the women?
2. What are they doing?
3. What foods do you see?
4. What foods do you usually buy?

PREPARING TO READ

1 UNDERSTANDING KEY VOCABULARY **Read the sentences. Write the words in bold next to the definitions.**

1 I enjoy a cup of hot tea in the afternoon. I add **honey**, not sugar, to make it sweet.

2 I play many **different** sports. I am on the soccer, basketball, and tennis teams.

3 My father **prepares** our family's dinner on weekends. He really likes cooking.

4 We buy our **bread** at a bakery. I enjoy it with butter and jam.

5 I have the **same** color eyes as my mother. They are dark gray.

6 There are five main **types** of food: grains, meats, fruits, vegetables, and dairy.

7 When it is hot outside, it is good to have water or other **drinks**.

a _____ (n) a basic food made from flour, water, and salt mixed together and baked

b _____ (adj) like something else

c _____ (adj) not like other things

d _____ (n) something that is part of a group of things that are like each other

e _____ (n) a sweet and sticky food made by bees

f _____ (n) a liquid that you drink, for example, water or soda

g _____ (v) to make something

2 USING YOUR KNOWLEDGE **Ask and answer the questions with a partner.**

1 What foods are popular all over the world?
2 Why do you think those foods are popular?
3 What are your favorite foods? Why?

3 PREVIEWING **Look at the title, photos, and headings on pages 126–127. Write *T* (true) or *F* (false) next to the statements. Then compare your answers with a partner.**

_____ 1 The text is from a website.

_____ 2 The text gives information and facts.

_____ 3 The text is a story of a person's travels around the world.

_____ 4 The text includes information about preparing tea.

TEA:
A WORLD HISTORY
BY A. CAPPER

INTRODUCTION: THE WORLD IN A TEACUP

1 Tea is tasty and good for you. It is also one of the most popular **drinks** around the world. But what is tea? And why is it so popular?

2 All tea comes from tea leaves, but tea is not always the **same**. There are many kinds of tea. You can drink black tea, green tea, white tea, or fruit tea. Each **type** of tea has a **different** taste and a different color.

3 The history of tea begins in Asia. In China, Korea, and Japan, tea is still very important today. In Japan, it can take many hours to **prepare** and drink tea with your guests. In Malaysia, a popular drink at breakfast is *teh tarik* ("pulled tea"). Malaysians say it is good for you and tastes good with *roti canai* – a kind of **bread**.

4 Tourists in Kuala Lumpur like watching the tea sellers make "pulled tea." The tea sellers pour hot water on black tea. After five minutes, they add sugar and milk. Then they "pull" the tea – they pour the tea from one cup to another many times.

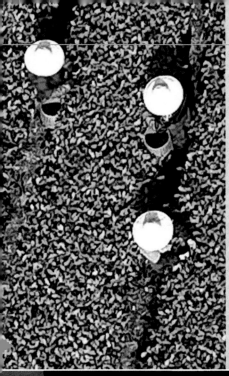

1.1 A tea seller prepares tea in Kuala Lumpur.

5 In many countries, you must have a special kettle[1] to make tea. People in different countries also like to add different things to their tea. For example, Russians use a special kettle called a *samovar*. They like drinking tea with lemon. Sometimes, they also drink tea with some sugar or jam. This makes it sweet.

> ❝ **What is tea? Why is it so popular?**❞

1.2 A Russian samovar

1.3 A Turkish Çaydanlık set

6 In Turkey, tea comes in a *Çaydanlık*. A *Çaydanlık* has two kettles: one for the water and one for the tea. Drink Turkish tea with some sugar.

7 Arab tea, called *karak*, is made with cardamom[2], ginger, milk, and sugar. In the United Kingdom, they add some milk and sugar. In the United States, tea is popular with **honey**.

8 The British usually eat cookies with their tea. They have specific times for drinking tea. There is "elevenses," which is tea served at 11:00 in the morning. They also have afternoon tea at 3:00 or 4:00.

[1]**kettle** (n) a container with a lid and a handle for boiling water

[2]**cardamom** (n) a South Asian plant with seeds used as a spice

4 READING FOR MAIN IDEAS **Read the text on pages 126–127. Match each main idea to the correct paragraph. Write the number from the text.**

_____ a People use special kettles to prepare tea.

_____ b The history of tea started in Asia.

_____ c There are different kinds of tea made from tea leaves.

_____ d In Kuala Lumpur, pulled tea is special.

_____ e Tea is very popular.

⚒ SKILLS

TAKING NOTES

When you take notes, you write down the important information from the text. Ask questions to help find this information. You do not need to write complete sentences in your notes. Use a chart to organize your ideas.

---

5 TAKING NOTES **Write information from the text in the chart.**

What country?	How is the tea prepared? What do people eat with it?
Malaysia	(1) Pour hot water on black tea. • After five minutes, add sugar and milk. • Then "pull" the tea. (Pour the tea from one cup to another many times.) • Eat roti canai with it.
Russia	(2)
Turkey	(3)
Arab countries	(4)
United Kingdom	(5)

6 SCANNING TO FIND INFORMATION **Scan the text. Write the names of the correct countries from the text in the blanks.**

1 People in _____ drink *teh tarik*.

2 In _____ , people prepare tea in a *samovar*.

3 People prepare tea for many hours in _____ .

4 Some people in _____ drink tea with sugar or jam.

5 People prepare tea with two kettles in _____ .

6 Tourists like watching tea sellers prepare tea in _____ .

☼ CRITICAL THINKING

7 **Work with a partner. Ask and answer the questions.**

APPLY

Do you prefer tea or coffee? Why?

APPLY

How do people drink tea in your country? (With sugar? With milk?)

ANALYZE

Why do you think people drink tea in so many countries?

☄ COLLABORATION

8 **A** Work in a small group. Create a survey to find out how people drink tea and what they eat with it. Write four more *yes/no* questions below.

Question	Yes	No
1 Do you drink tea with honey?		
2		
3		
4		
5		

B Ask at least three people your questions. Record their answers.

C Count the answers from each person in your group. Then write five sentences to summarize the results of your surveys. Share them with the class.

PREPARING TO READ

1 UNDERSTANDING KEY VOCABULARY **Read the sentences. Match the photos to the sentences using the words in bold.**

1   I eat **meat** for dinner. I like burgers or steak. _____

2   The restaurant always **serves** tea **with** a cookie. _____

3   I buy **vegetables** at the market in my city. _____

4   My dad is a fisherman, so we eat a lot of **fish**. _____

5   A popular **dish** for breakfast in the United States is pancakes. _____

6   In Mexico, beans and **rice** are popular. _____

7   I eat three **meals** a day: breakfast, lunch, and dinner. _____

2 USING YOUR KNOWLEDGE   **Work with a partner. Write different types of foods in the chart. Then take turns describing them.**

What foods do you like to eat in restaurants?	What foods do you like from your country?	What foods do you like from other countries?

3 PREVIEWING   **Look at the text and the photos on pages 132–133. Circle the correct options.**

1   The text is from a *website / book*.
2   The text is about different *types of food / things to do* in Melbourne.
3   The text is for *tourists / students*.
4   A cuisine is a *type of food / place to visit*.
5   The text *gives / does not give* opinions.

Home | The city | Map | Public transportation | Culture | Entertainment | Help

10 OF THE BEST BY CUISINE

1   You'll find the world in Melbourne! Learn about the best of every cuisine[1]. Warning: Do not read if you're hungry!

kabsa

Arab cuisine

Australian cuisine

American cuisine

Cambodian cuisine

Chinese cuisine

French cuisine

Japanese cuisine

Korean cuisine

Mexican cuisine

Turkish cuisine

Arab cuisine

2   At an Arab restaurant, you can find delicious **meat dishes**. Two popular dishes are *shawarma* and *kabsa*. *Shawarma* is a savory[2] meat dish. The meat is served in *pita* bread with **vegetables**. *Kabsa* is a popular **meal** in many Middle Eastern countries, but it is very popular in Saudi Arabia. *Kabsa* is a dish with **rice**, meat, and vegetables. There are many different ways to prepare *kabsa*. If you like meat dishes, you will enjoy your meal at an Arab restaurant.

3   In addition to the many flavorful meat dishes, Arab cuisine has many delicious vegetable dishes. *Falafel* is …

Read more ▶

Australian cuisine

4   If you are in Australia, you must try a crocodile or kangaroo dish! Many Australian restaurants serve crocodile curry. Crocodile meat is tasty and very good for you. (It is better that you eat crocodile than a crocodile eats you!) Kangaroo meat is also good for you. Kangaroo burgers are served on a type of bread. Australian restaurants also serve great fish and many other dishes …

crocodile curry

Read more ▶

Cambodian cuisine

5   At a Cambodian restaurant, there are many types of dishes. Cambodians like **fish** with rice. Cambodian dishes are **served with** a lot of vegetables. They are very popular in Cambodian cuisine. One famous dish is *amok trey*. Cambodians prepare *amok trey* with fish, nuts, coconut milk, and egg. There are many tasty dishes, but this is one of the best …

amok trey

Read more ▶

¹cuisine (n) a style of cooking

²savory (adj) food that is salty or spicy and not sweet

4 SCANNING TO FIND INFORMATION **Scan the text on pages 132–133. Write *T* (true) or *F* (false) next to the statements. Correct the false statements.**

_____ 1 The list of different cuisines is in alphabetical order.

_____ 2 *Shawarma* is a fish dish.

_____ 3 *Amok trey* is an Australian dish.

_____ 4 Kangaroo meat is popular in Australian restaurants.

_____ 5 Meat is popular in Arab cuisines.

_____ 6 There are different types of *kabsa*.

_____ 7 Kangaroo burgers are served on rice.

5 READING FOR DETAILS **Read the questions and the text. Underline the key words in the text. Then write the answers to the questions.**

1 Where is *kabsa* a very popular dish?

_____

2 Which dishes are served in or on bread?

_____

3 Which kinds of meat are good for you?

_____

4 Which cuisines have rice dishes?

_____

5 Which cuisines have fish dishes?

_____

☼ CRITICAL THINKING

6 SYNTHESIZING **Work with a partner. Use ideas from Reading 1 and Reading 2 to answer the questions.**

UNDERSTAND	APPLY	EVALUATE
What type of food is in all the cuisines in Reading 2?	What dishes and drinks from the readings do you want to try? Why?	Why do different countries have special ways of preparing food and drinks?

✤ COLLABORATION

7 **A** Work in small groups. Choose a dish or drink from Reading 1 or Reading 2. Brainstorm and write words in the idea map to describe it. Do not write the name of the dish or drink.

What is it made of?   What does it taste like?

What is it served with?

B Share your idea map with another group. Can they guess your dish?

C Repeat step B with other groups. At the end of the exercise, write the name of the dish in the middle circle of the idea map.

VOCABULARY ABOUT FOOD

 1 **Choose the word or phrase that has the same meaning as the word in bold.**

1 Tea is a **popular** drink all over the world.
   a well liked
   b interesting

2 *Amok trey* is a **tasty** dish from Cambodia.
   a nice
   b fish

3 *Amok trey* is **made with** fish, nuts, coconut milk, and egg.
   a prepared with
   b tastes like

4 Sugar makes tea taste **sweet**.
   a delicious, like honey
   b salty

5 *Shawarma* is **served in** pita bread.
   a comes inside
   b tastes like

6 In Great Britain, tea is often **served with** cookies.
   a cooked with
   b comes with

7 Meat dishes are **savory**.
   a sweet and sugary
   b salty and spicy

8 Fish is **good for** you. People who eat fish live longer.
   a has a good effect on your body
   b tastes good and sweet to you

9 Some people don't like **spicy** food. The taste is too strong and hot.
   a with strong flavors from spices, like cardamom, ginger, chili, etc.
   b food that is hard to bite and eat

COUNT AND NONCOUNT NOUNS

LANGUAGE

Count nouns name things you can count, such as vegetables, drinks, and meals. They can have a singular or a plural form and a singular or a plural verb.

singular	plural
One **vegetable is** cabbage.	**Vegetables are** served in *pita* bread.
A popular **dish is** *shawarma*.	Two popular **dishes are** *shawarma* and *kabsa*.

Noncount nouns have a singular form and a singular verb. They do not have a plural form or use a plural verb.

Fish is good for you. ~~Fishes are good for you~~.

Rice is served with many Indian dishes. ~~Rices are served with many Indian dishes~~.

2 **Read the sentences. Put a check (✓) if they are correct and an *X* if they are wrong. Use a dictionary to help you.**

_____ 1 Honeys are sweet.

_____ 2 Vegetables are popular in European cuisine.

_____ 3 Milks are good for children.

_____ 4 Bread are tasty.

_____ 5 Cookies are served with tea.

_____ 6 Burgers are served on a type of bread.

_____ 7 Fish are good for you.

_____ 8 Water is served in a glass.

3 **Correct the wrong sentences in Exercise 2.**

_____

_____

_____

_____

WATCH AND LISTEN

1 Arreau   2   3   4

PREPARING TO WATCH

1 ACTIVATING YOUR KNOWLEDGE **Work with a partner and answer the questions.**

1 What kinds of food come from cows? Which ones do you like?

2 Does your country have a national dish? Describe it.

2 PREDICTING CONTENT USING VISUALS **Look at the pictures from the video. Choose the correct word to complete the sentences.**

1 This is a French *city / village.*

2 People *cook / sell* food in the square.

3 The goats live *on a farm / in a zoo.*

4 The man is making *fruit / cheese.*

WHILE WATCHING

▶ **3** UNDERSTANDING MAIN IDEAS **Watch the video. Check (✓) the true statements.**

1 ☐ The village of Arreau is in the south of France.

2 ☐ The south of France is very rainy.

3 ☐ Cheese is very popular in France.

4 ☐ People can learn how to make cheese at the Tuchans' farm.

5 ☐ They get milk from the goats once a day.

(▶) **4** UNDERSTANDING DETAILS   **Watch again. Answer the questions.**

1   What do farmers sell in the market? _____

2   What does Mrs. Tuchan sell? _____

3   How much milk can a goat make every day? _____

4   How long does the cheese stay in the room? _____

5 MAKING INFERENCES   **Match the sentence halves.**

1   The farmers have to   a   like cheese.

2   Making cheese   b   have traditional foods.

3   Most French people   c   take care of the goats.

4   Most countries   d   takes time.

☼ CRITICAL THINKING

6 **Work with a partner and answer the questions.**

REMEMBER	APPLY	ANALYZE
What are the steps for making goat cheese?	What can you buy in outdoor markets in your country?	How do you think other kinds of cheese are made?

🐾 COLLABORATION

7 **A**   Work with a partner. On a piece of paper, write each word or phrase: *sweet, savory, good for you, tasty, popular,* and *spicy*. Then write two dishes to match each description.

B   Look at the foods on your paper. Take turns explaining how they are prepared and what they are usually served with.

C   Choose one dish per group to tell the class about. Take notes on the steps to prepare it. Use the video as a model. Tell the class about the dish, and show them a photo.

TRANSPORTATION

Key Reading Skill	Skimming
Additional Reading Skills	Understanding key vocabulary; previewing; scanning to find information; reading for details; using your knowledge; reading for main ideas; annotating; synthesizing
Language Development	Quantifiers; transportation collocations

ACTIVATE YOUR KNOWLEDGE

Work with a partner. Ask and answer the questions.

1 How do people in this city get to work and school?

2 Which way looks the fastest? Why?

3 How do you travel to work and school? Why?

PREPARING TO READ

1 UNDERSTANDING KEY VOCABULARY **Read the sentences. Choose the best definition for the word or phrase in bold.**

1 The **traffic** is moving slowly. There are a lot of cars on the road.
   a the cars, trucks, etc., driving on the road
   b the time it takes to get somewhere

2 When does the **train** get into the station? I need to be at work by 9 a.m.
   a a long, thin type of car that travels on tracks
   b a route or way for traveling from one place to another

3 I take the **subway** to work. I only have to go two stops.
   a a place for people to walk along the road
   b trains that travel underground, usually in a city

4 Many children learn to ride **bikes**. It's a fun and easy way to travel.
   a a type of transportation with two wheels that you sit on and move by turning two pedals
   b a type of transportation with four wheels and an engine.

5 I paid a **taxi** driver to take me from the airport to the city.
   a a place for planes to land and people to get on planes
   b a car with a driver who you pay to take you somewhere

6 My son takes the **bus** to school with other kids from his class.
   a a big type of car that takes many people around a city
   b a small car with three wheels

7 People don't ride **motorcycles** where I live. It is rainy, and they don't want to get wet.

    a a big bike with an engine for one or two people

    b railway tracks for moving things

8 In cities, there are many **transportation** choices. You can take a bus, subway, car, or bike to work.

    a the things people use to move from one place to another

    b the people living in a certain area

2 PREVIEWING **Work with a partner. Look at the text on pages 144–145 and answer the questions.**

1 What type of text is this? _____

2 Why do people write this type of text? _____

    _____

3 What are the three different parts in this text? _____

    _____

4 Who will answer the questions in this text? _____

    _____

5 What will the writers do with the answers to these questions? _____

    _____

Have you been in a traffic jam?

143

Bangkok City Planning

TRANSPORTATION SURVEY[1]

Please answer the questions about **transportation** in Bangkok. Your answers will help us make our city better.

Check (☑) the correct boxes to answer the questions.

A. About you

A1 How old are you?
- ☐ 14–17
- ☐ 18–21
- ☐ 22–31
- ☑ 32–53
- ☐ older than 53

A2 I am:
- ☐ male
- ☑ female

A3 What do you do?
- ☐ study
- ☑ work

B. Travel

B1 How long is your trip to work or school?
- ☐ 5–15 minutes
- ☑ 15–45 minutes
- ☐ 45–60 minutes
- ☐ more than 1 hour

B2 How do you get to work or school?
- ☐ on foot[2]
- ☐ **bike**
- ☐ car
- ☐ tuk-tuk
- ☐ **motorcycle**
- ☐ water taxi
- ☐ **taxi**
- ☐ **bus**
- ☐ Sky**Train**
- ☑ **subway**

[1]survey (n) a set of questions people are asked to get information

[2]on foot (prep phr) if you go somewhere on foot, you walk there.

B3 How often do you use these types of transportation?

types of transportation	always	often	sometimes	not often	never
on foot	✔				
bike				✔	
car		✔			
motorcycle					✔
water taxi				✔	
taxi				✔	
bus			✔		
SkyTrain			✔		
subway		✔			

B4 Which type or types of transportation do you own?

I own a: ☐ bike   ☑ car   ☐ motorcycle   ☐ other: _____

C. Opinion

C1 Read the statements in the chart. Do you agree or disagree with them?

statements	strongly agree	agree	neither agree nor disagree	disagree	strongly disagree
There is a lot of **traffic** in Bangkok.	✔				
The traffic makes me late.		✔			
We need more public transportation.	✔				

C2 Write any comments or suggestions that you have about transportation in Bangkok.

We should build more subway lines. Then more people could use the subway, and there would not be so much traffic on the roads.

Thank you for taking the time to answer the questions in this survey.

Need a ride?
Get a
tuk-tuk

WATER TAXI
Click here for
schedule and tickets.

SKIMMING

Skimming is useful when you want to understand what a text is about. When you skim, you look for the main ideas in a text and ignore the details. Main ideas are usually found at the beginning of paragraphs.

3 SKIMMING **Skim the text on pages 144–145. What information is the survey asking about? Circle the correct topics below.**

1 the number of hours people in Bangkok work or study
2 how people travel in Bangkok
3 the cost of transportation in Bangkok
4 popular forms of transportation in Bangkok
5 how people in Bangkok travel on vacation
6 what forms of transportation people own

4 SCANNING TO FIND INFORMATION **Scan the text for the survey answers.**

1 How old is the person? _____

2 How long is the person's trip? _____

3 How does the person travel to work? _____

4 What does the person never use for transportation? _____

5 Does the person think the traffic makes her late? _____

5 READING FOR DETAILS **Read the text. Write *T* (true) or *F* (false). Correct the false statements.**

_____ 1 There is not a place for people to write their suggestions in the survey.

_____ 2 The survey asks if the person is male or female.

_____ 3 The purpose of the survey is to see how people like Bangkok.

_____ 4 The person answering the survey often takes the bus.

_____ 5 The person answering the survey thinks more water taxis should be added.

CRITICAL THINKING

6 Work with a partner. Ask and answer the questions.

APPLY

What types of transportation do people usually use in your city or town?

EVALUATE

Which types of transportation are the best and which are the worst for:

a long trips?

b getting in shape and being healthy?

c places with no roads?

d families?

COLLABORATION

7 A Work in a small group. Create a survey to find out about transportation in your city. Write 5–10 questions. Use the survey in Reading 1 as an example.

B Each person in the group should survey five people and take notes on their answers.

C Look at the answers as a group. Summarize the results. Answer the following questions in your summary.

- How many people took the survey?
- How long do people spend going to work or school?
- How many people get to work or school with each type of transportation?
- How often do most people take each type of transportation?
- Which types of transportation do people have?

D Compare your summary with another group.

PREPARING TO READ

1 UNDERSTANDING KEY VOCABULARY **Use the words in the box to complete the sentences. Use the correct form. Some sentences have more than one answer.**

---

drive (v) to make a car, bus, or train move by controlling it

prefer (v) to like someone or something more than another person or thing

report (n) information about an event or situation

result (n) information that you get from something, like an exam, a survey, a medical test, etc.

ride (v) to travel by sitting in a car or train or on a bike

spend (v) to use time by doing something

take (v) to travel somewhere using a car, bus, or train

---

1 I _____ riding my bike to riding in a car. I like to be outside.

2 My mom _____ the bus to work every day. She gets there in ten minutes.

3 My dad _____ 40 minutes in traffic every morning. Driving in the morning takes a lot of time.

4 The traffic _____ said that traffic was moving slowly all over the city.

5 I got the _____ back from my test. I did great!

6 The bus driver _____ too fast! He should go more slowly on these busy streets.

7 I _____ the subway into the city on the weekends. It's nice not to drive.

Water taxis in Bangkok, Thailand

2 USING YOUR KNOWLEDGE **You are going to read a report in Reading 2. A report is a description of something or information about something. Work with a partner to complete the chart with ideas. Think of a different type of report in the third row.**

report	information	example
weather report	information about the weather for the day or week	daily temperature and weather description
news report		

3 PREVIEWING **Look at the report on pages 150–151. Write short answers to the questions. Compare your answers with a partner.**

1 What are the headings? _____

2 What is the main topic? _____

3 What does the report share? _____

4 What does Figure 1 show? _____

TRANSPORTATION IN *BANGKOK*

Introduction

1 This **report** shows the **results** of a survey about transportation in Bangkok. Over eight million people live in the city. The pie chart (Figure 1) shows the most popular types of transportation in Bangkok. It shows the percentage[1] of people who use each type of transportation to get to work or school.

Public Transportation

2 Every day, thousands of people use public and private transportation. A popular form of public transportation is the SkyTrain. People take public transportation so they don't have to drive themselves. Twenty-one percent of the population of Bangkok takes the SkyTrain to work or school. Another form of public transportation in the city is the bus. Eighteen percent of people who live in Bangkok **take** buses. People **prefer** buses to tuk-tuks because buses cost less money. Only 8% of people use tuk-tuks to get to work or school.

[1]**percentage** (n) how many out of 100

The busy Bangkok SkyTrain

Private Transportation

3 Most people in Bangkok use private transportation. They **drive** their own cars. Fourteen percent of people **ride** motorcycles to get to work or take children to school. Only 3% walk to work, and only 2% bike to work. Most places of work are too far away to walk or bike to.

Traffic

4 There is a lot of traffic in Bangkok. The roads are full of different types of vehicles[2] (cars, motorcycles, tuk-tuks, etc.). Twenty-three percent of people drive a car to work or school. Most people **spend** more than one hour every day traveling because the traffic is so bad. Almost 35% of people are late because of traffic jams. However, there are no traffic jams on the river. Eleven percent of people take the water taxi.

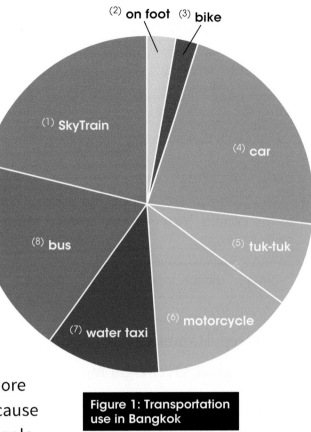

Figure 1: Transportation use in Bangkok

[2]**vehicles** (n) things such as cars or buses that take people from one place to another, especially using roads

4 SCANNING TO FIND INFORMATION **Scan the report on pages 150–151. Write the correct numbers in the blanks for the types of transportation in Figure 1.**

1 _____%   5 _____%

2 _____%   6 _____%

3 _____%   7 _____%

4 _____%   8 _____%

5 READING FOR MAIN IDEAS **Read the report. Write the words and phrases from the box in the blanks. You can use a word more than once. You may have to change a verb form.**

drive   motorcycles   take   traffic   transportation

This report shows the results of a survey about (1) _____ in Bangkok. Over eight million people live in Bangkok. The pie chart (Figure 1) shows the most popular types of transportation in Bangkok. It shows the percentage of people who use each type of transportation to get to work or school. Twenty-one percent of the population of Bangkok (2) _____ the SkyTrain to work or school. Another way to travel is to (3) _____ the bus. However, it is more popular to (4) _____ your own car. There is a lot of (5) _____ in Bangkok. The roads are full of cars, (6) _____, etc.

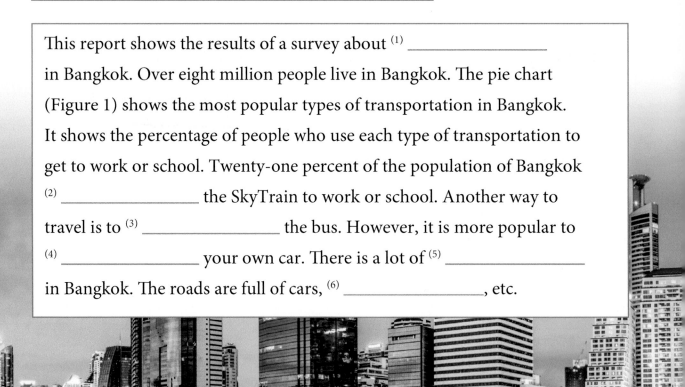

6 ANNOTATING **Read the report again. Find and underline the information that answers the questions. Then use your notes to write the answers.**

1 How many people live in Bangkok?

_____

2 Is the SkyTrain a public or private form of transportation?

_____

3 What percentage of people drive cars?

_____

4 How long do most people spend in traffic?

_____

5 What percentage of people are late because of traffic jams?

_____

💡 CRITICAL THINKING

7 SYNTHESIZING **Work with a partner. Use ideas from Reading 1 and Reading 2 to answer the questions.**

APPLY

What is the most popular way to get to work in Bangkok? Why do you think that is?

ANALYZE

If you lived in Bangkok, what transportation would you use? Why?

EVALUATE

Why is it important for cities to know how people get to work?

👥 COLLABORATION

8 A Work in a small group. Make a pie chart about transportation in your city. Use Figure 1 on page 151 as an example. Use the information in your surveys from Exercise 7 on page 147 to complete the pie chart.

B Compare your information with another group. If you can, go online to check the information, and make changes to your chart.

C Think about the results. Why are some forms of transportation more popular? Write three statements to explain the information in your chart. Then present your pie chart and reasons to the class.

QUANTIFIERS

LANGUAGE

Quantifiers tell you the answer to the question *How many?* Use quantifiers before a noun. For small numbers, use *a few, not many,* and *some.* For bigger numbers, use *many, a lot of,* and *most.*

no	not many / a few	some	many / a lot of	most	all

0%   100%

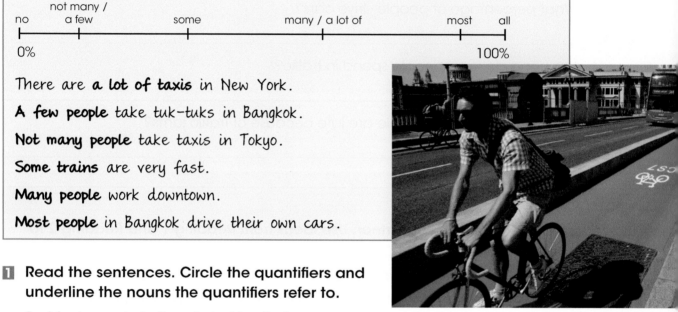

There are **a lot of taxis** in New York.

A few people take tuk-tuks in Bangkok.

Not many people take taxis in Tokyo.

Some trains are very fast.

Many people work downtown.

Most people in Bangkok drive their own cars.

1 **Read the sentences. Circle the quantifiers and underline the nouns the quantifiers refer to.**

1 Most people in Bangkok drive their own cars.
2 Some people ride motorcycles.
3 Not many people bike to work or school.
4 A few people take the water taxi.
5 Many people take the SkyTrain.

2 **Read the sentences and write quantifiers in the blanks. Use the percentages to help you. More than one answer is possible.**

1 _____ (*62%*) people in London take the subway to work.

2 _____ (*8%*) people drive their cars to work in London.

3 Today, _____ (*18%*) people in London bike to work.

4 _____ (*9%*) people in London take the bus to work.

5 _____ (*3%*) people in London walk or run to work.

TRANSPORTATION COLLOCATIONS

LANGUAGE

You can use these types of collocations when you talk about transportation.

subject	verb	determiner	noun (transportation)	prepositional phrase (*to* + place)
Many students People	take	the / their / a	bus / subway / cars / taxi	to school. to work.
My parents	drive	their / a	car	to work.
I	ride	the / a	bus / subway / bike / motorcycle	to school.

subject	verb	prepositional phrase (*to* + place)	prepositional phrase (*by* + noun for transportation)
Many students People	travel get	to school to work	by bus. by subway. by car.

3 **Put the words in order to make sentences.**

1 to / take / school / We / a bus / .

_____

2 travels / by / work / train / Melissa / to / .

_____

3 takes / to / the city / his car / Shu / .

_____

4 get to / work / Many people / motorcycle / by / .

_____

4 **Work with a partner. Ask and answer questions with the verbs *take, drive, ride, travel,* and *get*.**

Do you ride the subway? How many people take the bus?

WATCH AND LISTEN

GLOSSARY

rider (n) a person who rides in a car, train, or bus, or on a bike or motorcycle
platform (n) the area in a train or subway station where you get on and off a train
attendant (n) someone whose job is to help people in a particular place
calm (adj) relaxed; not worried or excited

PREPARING TO WATCH

1 ACTIVATING YOUR KNOWLEDGE **Work with a partner and answer the questions.**

1   What are the most common types of transportation in your city?
2   What are some unusual types of transportation?
3   What cities have subway systems?

2 PREDICTING CONTENT USING VISUALS **Look at the pictures from the video. Circle the correct word.**

1   This train is *underground / over ground*.
2   Many people are waiting to get *on / off* the train.
3   The city is *busy / quiet*.
4   The man is helping people in the *shopping mall / subway station*.

WHILE WATCHING

3 UNDERSTANDING MAIN IDEAS **Watch the video. Write *T* (true) or *F* (false) next to the statements. Correct the false statements.**

_____ 1   Every day, millions of people travel on subways that are under the ground.

_____ 2   The oldest subway system is in Tokyo.

_____ 3   London's subway system is called the "Tube."

_____ 4   London has the busiest subway system.

_____ 5   Attendants help keep riders safe, calm, and on time.

▶ **4** UNDERSTANDING DETAILS **Watch again. Choose the correct answer.**

1 How many subway systems are in the world today?

    a over 500   b over 250   c over 150

2 How do 500,000 Londoners get to work each day?

    a They go by subway.   b They walk.   c They drive.

3 How many people take the Tokyo subway system every hour?

    a 3,500   b 35,000   c 350,000

5 MAKING INFERENCES **Complete the sentences with the words in the box.**

faster   helpful   traffic   usually

1 There is less _____ when people take the subway.

2 If you work in a city, subways are often _____ than cars.

3 People in Tokyo are _____ on time for work.

4 It is _____ to have an attendant on the subway platform.

☀ CRITICAL THINKING

6 **Work with a partner and answer the questions.**

APPLY	ANALYZE	EVALUATE
Have you traveled on the subway in London, Tokyo, New York City, or another large city? How was it?	Subways help people get to work. What are some other benefits of subways to cities?	What do you think are the best ways to travel in a city? Why?

🖧 COLLABORATION

7 **A** Work with a partner. Make a list of the three biggest transportation problems in your city. Then write five ways to make transportation in your city better.

    B Create a two-minute report. Present your report to the class. One person can discuss the problems, and the other can discuss the solutions. Be prepared to answers questions from the rest of the class.

GLOSSARY OF KEY VOCABULARY

Words that are part of the Academic Word List are noted with an Ⓐ in this glossary.

UNIT 1 PEOPLE

READING 1

city (n) a large town, such as Miami or Osaka

country (n) an area of land that has its own government, such as Canada or Slovakia

date of birth (n) the day you were born

hobby (n) an activity that you enjoy and do regularly

job Ⓐ (n) the work you do to get money

language (n) a type of communication used by the people of a particular country

READING 2

family (n) a group of people related to each other, such as a mother, a father, and their children

interested in (adj phr) wanting to learn more about something

live (v) to have your home somewhere

music (n) sounds that are made by playing instruments or singing

normal Ⓐ (adj) usual, ordinary, and expected

unusual (adj) different and not usual, often in a way that is interesting or exciting

watch (v) to look at something for some time

work (v) to do a job, especially the job you do to get money

UNIT 2 CLIMATE

READING 1

cold (adj) having a low temperature; not hot

fall (n) the season of the year between summer and winter when the leaves change color and fall from trees; autumn

spring (n) the season of the year between winter and summer, when the plants and trees begin to grow

summer (n) the season of the year when the weather is the warmest

warm (adj) having a temperature between cool and hot

winter (n) the season of the year when the weather is the coldest

READING 2

climate (n) the weather that a place usually has

cloudy (adj) with a lot of clouds

dry (adj) with very little or no rain or water

rainfall (n) the amount of rain that falls in one place

rainy (adj) with a lot of rain

season (n) one of the four periods of the year: winter, spring, summer, or fall

sunny (adj) with a lot of sun

windy (adj) with a lot of wind

UNIT 3 LIFESTYLE

READING 1

breakfast (n) the food you eat in the morning after you wake up

cook (v) to prepare food by heating it

dinner (n) the food you eat at the end of the day

get up (phr v) to rise from bed after sleeping

lunch (n) the food you eat in the middle of the day

meet (v) to see and speak to someone for the first time

swim (v) to move through water by moving your body

travel (v) to go from one place to another, usually over a long distance

READING 2

afternoon (n) the period of time between 12:00 p.m. and 5 p.m.

busy (adj) having a lot of things to do

evening (n) the period of time between 5:00 p.m. and 11:00 p.m.

morning (n) the period of time between 5:00 a.m. and 12:00 p.m.

relax Ⓐ (v) to become calm and comfortable

schedule Ⓐ (n) a list of planned activities or things that need to be done

weekday (n) Monday to Friday, when many people work

weekend (n) Saturday and Sunday, when many people do not work

UNIT 4 PLACES

READING 1

forest (n) a large area of trees growing closely together, such as the redwood forest in California

lake (n) a large area of fresh water that has land all around it, such as Lake Michigan

map (n) a picture that shows a place and the rivers, lakes, and other areas in it

mountain (n) a very high hill, such as Mount Everest

ocean (n) one of the five main areas of salt water on Earth, such as the Atlantic and Pacific

river (n) water that flows across the land to a bigger area of water, such as the Mississippi River

sea (n) a large area of salt water, such as the Mediterranean Sea

READING 2

beach (n) an area of sand or rocks next to a sea, ocean, or lake

capital (n) the most important city in a country, where the government is, such as Washington, D.C.

famous (adj) known by many people

international (adj) relating to or involving two or more countries

island (n) land with water all around it

modern (adj) made with new ideas and designs

popular (adj) liked by many people

tourist (n) a person who travels and visits places for fun

UNIT 5 JOBS

friendly (adj) nice and kind

healthy (adj) not sick; well

hospital (n) a place where people who are sick or hurt go for help

in shape (adj) in good health; strong

medicine (n) something you take to feel better

nurse (n) a person who helps doctors and takes care of people

pay (n) the money you receive for doing a job

pilot (n) a person who flies an airplane

READING 2

center (n) a place with a special purpose, such as a health center

company (n) an organization that sells something to make money

engineer (n) a person who designs and builds things

good at (adj) able to do something well

great (adj) very good; excellent

high school (n) a school for children about 15 to 18 years old, between middle school and college or university

interesting (adj) getting your attention because it is exciting; not boring

teacher (n) a person who helps others learn

UNIT 6 HOMES AND BUILDINGS

READING 1

garden (n) an area around a house with grass, flowers, or trees

glass (n) a hard, clear material that windows and bottles are made of

plastic (n) a material that is used in a lot of different ways, e.g. bags, toys, and cups

roof (n) the outside top of a building or vehicle

tall (adj) having a greater than normal height; not short

wall (n) one of the sides of a room or building

window (n) part of a wall that has glass in it, for letting in light and for looking through

wood (n) the hard material that trees are made of

READING 2

apartment (n) a set of rooms for someone to live in on one level of a building or house

building (n) a house, school, office, or store with a roof and walls

cheap (adj) costing little money; not expensive

cost (v) to have an amount of money as a price that someone must pay

elevator (n) a machine, like a small room, that carries people up or down in a tall building

expensive (adj) costing a lot of money; not cheap

UNIT 7 FOOD AND CULTURE

READING 1

bread (n) a basic food made from flour, water, and salt mixed together and baked
different (adj) not like other things
drink (n) a liquid that you drink, for example, water or soda
honey (n) a sweet and sticky food made by bees
prepare (v) to make something
same (adj) like something else; not different
type (n) something that is part of a group of things that are like each other; kind or sort

READING 2

dish (n) food that is prepared in a particular way
fish (n) an animal that lives in water and swims
meal (n) the food that you eat in the morning, afternoon, or evening (breakfast, lunch, and dinner)
meat (n) soft parts of animals, used as food
rice (n) small grains from a plant that are cooked and eaten
serve with (phr v) to give one type of food with another type of food
vegetable (n) plants used as food, such as carrots or spinach

UNIT 8 TRANSPORTATION

READING 1

bike (n) a type of transportation with two wheels that you sit on and move by turning two pedals (= parts you press with your feet); a bicycle
bus (n) a big type of car that takes many people around a city
motorcycle (n) a big bike with an engine for one or two people
subway (n) trains that travel underground, usually in a city
taxi (n) a car with a driver who you pay to take you somewhere
traffic (n) the cars, trucks, etc., driving on the road
train (n) a long, thin type of car that travels on tracks with people or things
transportation Ⓐ (n) the things people use to move themselves or things from one place to another, such as cars, buses, and trains

READING 2

drive (v) to make a car, bus, or train move by controlling it
prefer (v) to like someone or something more than another person or thing
report (n) information about an event or situation
result (n) information that you get from something, like an exam, a survey, a medical test, etc.
ride (v) to travel by sitting in a car or train or on a bike
spend (v) to use time by doing something
take (v) to travel somewhere using a car, bus, or train

VIDEO SCRIPTS

UNIT 1

▶ Thailand's Moken Fishermen

Narrator: This is Goon, and this is where he lives.

He lives in a village by the sea, on an island called Ko Surin. His island is near the west coast of Thailand in Asia.

Goon and his friends are part of the Moken people. They live on land, but they spend a lot of their time in and on the sea.

The Moken people are very good at sailing, fishing, and diving. But they don't use special equipment or goggles.

They jump from their boat into the water. These boys are very good swimmers.

But how can they see to find food underwater without goggles? Goon and his friends are special.

They can see everything underwater easily. Goon can see the beautiful fish and plants around him.

This helps him catch fish and other sea animals for his friends and family.

UNIT 2

▶ The Growing Ice Cap

Narrator: In the beginning of winter here, the days grow short and cold. Snow and cold temperatures move south into parts of North America, Europe, and Asia.

Winter is hard here. Water in the air, in rivers, and in plants turns to ice. As a result, most of the plants die. But some trees, like fir trees and pine trees, can live in very cold temperatures. These trees make up the greatest forest on Earth, called the *taiga*.

The taiga forest goes around the northern part of the Earth. From Alaska to Canada, from Scandinavia to Russia, it has almost 30% of all the trees on Earth!

During the winter, in the most northern part of the taiga forest, freezing air from the north meets warm air from the south. Heavy snow covers this area of the taiga until warmer temperatures return in the spring.

UNIT 3

▶ Panama's Kuna People

Narrator: The Kuna people live in Colombia and Panama. Almost 35,000 of them live on islands near the coast of Panama called Kuna Yala. They are people of the sea.

Many of the Kuna are fishermen. They sometimes swim more than 100 feet deep and stay underwater for two minutes at a time. They catch fish and lobsters for food.

They also get food from their islands. They grow coconuts on many of the smaller islands. Most of the people live in villages on the larger islands. They have a rich culture, and they wear colorful traditional clothes every day.

The Kuna always take care of their islands and keep their villages clean. Every morning they go to the beach and sweep the sand.

They have small gardens around their homes, and they water their plants every day. They also raise animals.

Music is important to the Kuna men, women, and children. In their free time, they often play music and dance. Their daily life is probably very different from yours and mine.

UNIT 4

▶ The *Cenotes* of Mexico

Narrator: In the southeast part of Mexico, known as the Yucatán, there are many rich, green forests.

Here, these amazing holes are the only spaces in the trees. They are very deep, they are made of rock, and they are often full of water. Mexicans call these places *cenotes*.

Olmo Torres-Talamante is a scientist. For him, the *cenotes* are very special. He studies them, and the plants and animals in and around them.

Water is very important in the Yucatán. It rains a lot here, but there are no lakes or rivers. When it rains, the water goes down into the rock under the Yucatán. Over time, it makes the *cenotes*.

Cenotes are the only places to find fresh water in the Yucatán. They help the animals and plants in the forest live.

Lily pads, fish, and turtles all live at the top of the *cenotes*, where it's warm and light.

But when Olmo swims deeper into the cave, it gets cold and dark. How can anything live here?

But even here, the scientist finds life.

UNIT 5

▶ Utah's Bingham Mine

Narrator: This is the Bingham copper mine in Utah, in the western United States. It's the largest mine of its kind in the world. And it gets bigger all the time. Today it's two-and-a-half miles wide and almost one mile deep.

Matt Lengerich is the operations manager of the mine.

It produces enough copper each year to make wires for every home in the USA and Mexico. We use copper everywhere—in our homes, cell phones, and cars—and some of it comes from here.

But the rocks contain only a small amount of copper. So Matt's workers have to dig up a lot of rocks to get enough copper. That's why Bingham mine is so big.

Matt's workers use these giant trucks to dig up the copper. Sometimes the copper is so deep that they have to dig for seven years to reach it.

Everything about the mine is big. These giant trucks are heavier than a jumbo jet and work 24 hours a day.

Drivers use the giant trucks to move the rocks and copper.

But they also use something stronger.

The Bingham mine is more than 100 years old, and it's larger than any other mine of its kind.

UNIT 6

▶ To Build the Tallest

Narrator: For almost 4,000 years the Great Pyramid of Egypt was the world's tallest building. It is 455 feet, or almost 140 meters, tall, and it is made of stone.

Then in the year 1311, a small town in Britain finally built something taller.

The Lincoln Cathedral was also made of stone, but its makers used new ways to build it taller. With the three tall spires on top, Lincoln Cathedral was 46 feet, or 14 meters, taller than the Great Pyramid.

To build taller than the pyramids and cathedrals, we needed a new material: steel. In 1887, the Eiffel Tower in Paris, France, became almost two times taller than the Lincoln Cathedral.

In 1930, the Chrysler Building in New York City, used steel to make it the tallest skyscraper in the world.

One year later, the Empire State Building used steel to go even higher.

The next big change was in 1972 when New York's very tall World Trade Center was finished.

One year later, the Sears Tower in Chicago, Illinois, opened. Steel and glass made these buildings light.

Later, the Petronas Towers in Kuala Lumpur, Malaysia, used steel, glass, and concrete.

At 1,667 feet tall, Taipei 101 in Taipei City was the first building to be half a kilometer high. And buildings like the Burj Khalifa in Dubai, in the United Arab Emirates, keep pushing higher.

UNIT 7

▶ Goat Cheese

Narrator: This is the village of Arreau in the south of France. Every Thursday morning in Arreau, there is a market. Here, farmers sell fruit, vegetables, bread, meat, and cheese.

Cheese is very popular in France. And Arreau has some very special cheese—goat cheese.

Mrs. Tuchan sells goat cheese from her farm.

Her farm is in a village near Arreau. People can visit the farm to learn how she and her husband make cheese.

First they have to get the milk from the goats. The goats wait at the door. They go into the milking room one by one. Mrs. Tuchan uses a machine to get the milk. She does this twice a day. Each goat can give more than two quarts of milk every day.

Next, the milk goes to a different room – the cheese-making room.

Now they have to turn the milk into cheese. Mr. Tuchan adds an ingredient to the goat milk. Then, he puts it in small plastic cups with holes in the bottom.

The next day, he turns the cheese over. Then he adds some salt to it.

Next, he moves the cheese to another room. The cheese stays here for one to three weeks. Then it will be ready to sell, and to eat.

UNIT 8

▶ Modern Subways

Narrator: How do people in big cities travel? Many of them take the subway. Subways move millions of people underground every day. There are over 150 subway systems in the world today.

The oldest one is in London, England. There, everyone calls it the "Tube."

At 8:00 a.m., the Tube really gets busy. In the morning, over 500,000 Londoners go to work by subway. Of course, people on the streets can't see them.

But what if the Tube ran above the ground?

Every day in London, over 500 trains on 250 miles of track move nearly 3 million people.

That's a lot of people, but the busiest subway system in the world is in Tokyo, Japan.

There are more people in Tokyo than in any other city in the world. Around 35,000 people take the Tokyo subway every hour. That means 8 million riders travel underground every day.

On every platform, there are 25 subway attendants, like Yuhei Mitsuhashi.

They keep the riders safe, calm, and on time, because the trains cannot be late.

CREDITS

The authors and publishers acknowledge the following sources of copyright material and are grateful for the permissions granted. While every effort has been made, it has not always been possible to identify the sources of all the material used, or to trace all copyright holders. If any omissions are brought to our notice, we will be happy to include the appropriate acknowledgements on reprinting.

The publisher has used its best endeavors to ensure that the URLs for external websites referred to in this book are correct and active at the time of going to press. However, the publisher has no responsibility for the websites and can make no guarantee that a site will remain live or that the content is or will remain appropriate.

Photo Credits
The publishers are grateful to the following for permission to reproduce copyright photographs and material:

Key: T = Top, C = Center, B = Below, L = Left, R = Right, TL = Top Left, TR = Top Right, BL = Below Left, BR = Below Right, CL = Center Left, CR = Center Right

The following images are sourced from Getty Images.

pp. 14-15: Mitchell Funk; p. 16 (L): Maridav/Istock; p. 16 (C): Hero Images; p. 16 (R): Nicolasmccomber/E+; p. 17 (inset): Peter Cade/Digitalvision; p. 17 (B): Indranil Mukherjee/Afp; pp. 18-19: Thomas Gloning/Moment; p. 18 (inset): Jim Mcisaac; p. 19 (T): Maury Phillips; p. 19 (BR): Stringer/Apf; p. 19 (BL): Abbie Parr; p. 20: Katsumi Kasahara/Gamma-Rapho; pp. 22-23: John Lawson/Belhaven/Moment; p. 22 (C): Klaus Vedfelt/Taxi; p. 24 (L): Bernd Thissen/Dpa; pp. 24-25 (B): Marka/Universal Images Group; p. 25 (TR): Ibrahim Yakut/Anadolu Agency; pp. 26-27 (B): Nejdetduzen/Moment; p. 28: Hill Street Studios/Blend Images; p. 30: Pius99/Istock; p. 31: Taylor Weidman/Lightrocket; pp. 32-33: Daniel_Kay/Istock; p. 34 (A): Trinette Reed/Blend Images; p. 34 (B): Diane Cook/Len Jenshel/The Image Bank; p. 34 (C): James O'Neil/Stone; p. 34 (D): Nikolajtr/Room; p. 34 (BR): Jake Norton/Aurora; p. 35 (CL): Amos Chapple/Lonely Planet Images; p. 35 (BL): Amos Chapple/Lonely Planet Images; p. 35 (CR): Bernhard Lang/Photonica; p. 36: Dmitry Feoktistov/Tass; p. 37 (TR): Olivier Renck/Aurora; p. 37 (CR): Bill Bachmann/First Light; p. 37 (BR): Amos Chapple/Lonely Planet Images; p. 39: Lartal/The Image Bank; p. 40 (A): Oliver Rossi/The Image Bank; p. 40 (B): James Osmond/The Image Bank; p. 40 (C): Peter De Rooij/Moment; p. 40 (D): Warren Faidley/Corbis; pp. 40-41 (B): Kriangkrai Thitimakorn/Moment; p. 42 (T): M.M. Sweet/Moment; p. 42 (CR): Omersukrugoksu/E+; p. 42 (BR): Harvepino/Istock; p. 43 (BL): Lola L. Falantes/Moment Open; p. 43 (BR): Jacquesvandinteren/Istock; pp. 44-45: Franckjoseph/E+; p. 46: Amos Chapple/Lonely Planet Images; p. 48 (T): Kim Schandorff; pp. 50-51: Aleksandarnakic/E+; p. 52 (CL): Westend61; p. 52 (CR): Viewstock; p. 52 (BL): Sturti/Istock; p. 52 (BR): Peopleimages/E+; pp. 52-53: Jacob Ammentorp Lund/Istock; pp. 54-55: Mangiwau/Moment; p. 54 (BR): John Noble/Lonely Planet Images; p. 55 (CL): Johnny Haglund/Lonely Planet Images; p. 55 (CR): John Noble/Lonely Planet Images; p. 56: Marc Dozier/Corbis Documentary; p. 58: Doug Menuez/Forrester Images/Photodisc; pp. 60-61: Bravissimos/Istock; p. 60 (TL): Kevin C. Cox; p. 60 (TR): Uschools/E+; p. 61 (BR): Wavebreakmedia Ltd; pp. 62-63: Jeff Greenberg/Universal Images Group; pp. 64-65: Hero Images; p. 66 (T): Georgette Douwma/Photographer'S Choice; pp. 68-69: M Swiet Productions/Moment; pp. 70-71: Eye Ubiquitous/Universal Images Group; p. 71 (BR): Franckreporter/E+; p. 72: Ian Cuming/Ikon Images; p. 73 (T) UniversalImagesGroup/Getty Images; p. 73 (BR): De Agostini/G. Dagli Orti/De Agostini Picture Library; p. 75: Cartarium/Istock; p. 76: John Coletti/Photolibrary; p. 78: Ishara S.Kodikara/Stringer/Afp; pp. 78-79: Photogerson/Istock; p. 79: Buena Vista Images/Photodisc; p. 81: Dea/G. Sosio/De Agostini; p. 84: Tetra Images; pp. 86-87: Monty Rakusen/Cultura; p. 88: Portra Images/Taxi; p. 89 (BL): Image Source/Digitalvision; p. 89 (BR): Ryan Mcvay/The Image Bank; p. 90 (B): Jose Fuste Raga/Corbis Documentary; pp. 90-91: David Lees/The Image Bank; p. 90 (TR): Arctic-Images/Taxi; p. 90 (BR): Rolf Hicker Photography/All Canada Photos;

p. 92: Blaine Harrington Iii/Corbis Documentary; p. 94: Alexander Hassenstein; p. 95 (T): Hill Street Studios/Blend Images; p. 95 (B): Cultura Exclusive/J J D; p. 96: Rosa Kavanagh/Corbis Documentary; pp. 96-97: Ralf Hiemisch/Fstop; p. 97 (TL): Nic Lehoux/Corbis Documentary; p. 97 (BL): Multi-Bits/Taxi; p. 99: Peter Cook/Corbis Documentary; p. 100: Wayne Hutchinson/Corbis Documentary; p. 102: Gadtan Rossier/Moment; pp. 104-105: Xose Manuel Casal Luis/Moment; pp. 106-107: Johner Images; p. 106 (A): Blair_Witch/Istock; p. 106 (B): Kcconsulting/Istock; p. 106 (C): Schantalao/Istock; p. 106 (D): S.B. Nace/Lonely Planet Images; p. 106 (E): Jamie Grill/Iconica; p. 106 (F): Future Light/Photolibrary; p. 106 (G): Peter Starman/Photographer'S Choice Rf; p. 106 (H): Zsolt Bute/Eyeem; p. 108 (T): Jetta Productions/Iconica; p. 108 (B): View Pictures/Universal Images Group; p. 109 (TR): Deconphotostudio; p. 109 (CR): Architecture: Lada Hrsak And Danielle Huls, Photography ©Thomas Landen; p. 111: Bdsklo/Istock Editorial; p. 112 (BL): View Pictures/Contributor/Universal Images Group; p. 112 (BR): View Pictures/Contributor/Universal Images Group; pp. 112-113: Rick Friedman/Corbis News; p. 113 (BR): Stereostok/Istock; p. 114: Gionnixxx/Istock; p. 115 (TR): Gavin Hellier/Awl Images; p. 115 (BR): Ed Norton/Lonely Planet Images; pp. 116-117: Anna Shtraus/Moment; p. 118: George Rose; p. 120: Anucha Sirivisansuwan/Moment; pp. 122-123: Tamvisut/Moment; p. 124 (BL): Pretti/Istock; p. 124 (BR): Debby Lewis-Harrison/Cultura; p. 125: Garo/Canopy; p. 126: Visual China Group/Contributor; p. 126 (BL): Carlina Teteris/Moment; p. 127 (BL): Gaza Press/Rex/Shutterstock; p. 127 (TR): Danita Delimont/Gallo Images; pp. 128-129: Andia/Universal Images Group; p. 130 (a): Antonio Ciufo/Moment Open; p. 130 (b): Kai Stiepel/Stockfood Creative; p. 130 (c): Edo73/Istock; p. 130 (d): Bridget Davey/Moment Mobile; p. 130 (e): Julia_Sudnitskaya/Istock; p. 130 (f): Kelvin Kam/Eyeem; p. 130 (g): Jennifer Levy/Stockfood Creative; p. 131: Will Heap © Dorling Kindersley; p. 132 (CR): Hisham Ibrahim/Moment Mobile; p. 133 (BL): Martin Robinson/Lonely Planet Images; pp. 132-133: James O'Neil/Stone; p. 133 (TL): Maejitr/Istock; pp. 134-135: Didier Marti/Moment Open; p. 136: Tatiana Dyuvbanova/Eyeem; p. 137: Runphoto/The Image Bank; p. 138: Jtb Photo/Universal Images Group; pp. 140-141: Naufal Mq/Moment; p. 142: Dan Kitwood; p. 143: Amit Goldstein/Eyeem; p. 144: Worawut Charoen/Eyeem; p. 145 (BL): Will Gray/Awl Images; p. 145 (BR): Joel Carillet/E+; p. 147: Patrick Fraser/Photolibrary; pp. 148-149: Garden Photo World/David C Phillips/Canopy; p. 150: Akabei/Istock Editorial; pp. 152-153: Sirintra Pumsopa/Moment; p. 154: Mike Kemp/Corbis Historical; p. 156: Pawel Libera/Photolibrary.

Illustrations
by Martin Sanders (Beehive Illustration) p. 79; Rudolf Farkas (Beehive Illustration) p. 83.

Video Supplied by BBC Worldwide Learning.

Video Stills Supplied by BBC Worldwide Learning.

Corpus
Development of this publication has made use of the Cambridge English Corpus (CEC). The CEC is a multi-billion word computer database of contemporary spoken and written English. It includes British English, American English, and other varieties of English. It also includes the Cambridge Learner Corpus, developed in collaboration with the University of Cambridge ESOL Examinations. Cambridge University Press has built up the CEC to provide evidence about language use that helps produce better language teaching materials.

Cambridge Dictionaries
Cambridge dictionaries are the world's most widely used dictionaries for learners of English. The dictionaries are available in print and online at dictionary.cambridge.org. Copyright © Cambridge University Press, reproduced with permission.

Typeset by QBS

Audio by John Marshall Media

INFORMED BY TEACHERS

Classroom teachers shaped everything about *Prism*. The topics. The exercises. The critical thinking skills. Everything. We are confident that *Prism* will help your students succeed in college because teachers just like you helped guide the creation of this series.

Prism Advisory Panel

The members of the *Prism* Advisory Panel provided inspiration, ideas, and feedback on many aspects of the series. *Prism* is stronger because of their contributions.

Gloria Munson
University of Texas, Arlington

Dinorah Sapp
University of Mississippi

Kim Oliver
Austin Community College

Christine Hagan
George Brown College/Seneca College

Wayne Gregory
Portland State University

Heidi Lieb
Bergen Community College

Julaine Rosner
Mission College

Stephanie Kasuboski
Cuyahoga Community College

GLOBAL INPUT

Teachers from more than 500 institutions all over the world provided valuable input through:
- Surveys
- Focus Groups
- Reviews